CROCHET SCANDINAVIAN Christmas Gnomes

Photographs: frechverlag GmbH, 70839 Gerlingen; lichtpunkt GmbH, Michael Ruder
Illustrations by schwab:illustrationen, Ursula Schwab, Haselund with the following exception:
© cienpies/iStock/Getty Images: (Scandinavian border)
Art Director: Lisa Schreiber
Art Producer: Stacey Stambaugh
Production Editor: Rachel Taenzler
Production Designer: Martin Worthington

Published by Callisto Publishing LLC C/O Sourcebooks LLC
P.O. Box 4410, Naperville, Illinois 60567-4410
(630) 961-3900
callistopublishing.com

"Christmas Crochet" by Annelie Kojic was first published in 2023 under the title "Weihnachtliche Wichtelhäkelei" by frechverlag GmbH, an imprint of Penguin Random House Verlagsgruppe GmbH, Munich, Germany. Translated from German by Ulatus.

Library of Congress Cataloging-in-Publication Data is on file with the publisher.

Printed and bound in China.
WKT 10 9 8 7 6 5 4 3 2 1

CROCHET SCANDINAVIAN Christmas Gnomes

Miniatures for the Mischievous Gnome in Your Home

ANNELIE KOJIC

Hello!

The most wonderful time of the year is almost upon us once more - Christmas is just around the corner! In recent years, it has become increasingly popular for people to adorn their houses and apartments with little homemade doors. It is said that behind these doors dwell tiny beings that go by various names, but most of us would recognize them as gnomes.

In this book, I will show you how you can crochet your own cute little Christmas gnomes and transform your home into a winter wonderland. And to make sure your new friends have no trouble making themselves comfortable, you can fashion all kinds of accessories for them out of yarn. There's a mailbox for the gnomes' notes, boots for walks in the snow, and a sofa they can use to relax after a tiring day of playing pranks - everything they need.

And of course, it wouldn't be Christmas without some delicious baked goods! That's why I've also put together some instructions to help you crochet baking equipment and ingredients, such as a mixing bowl, eggs, pot holders, and more for your gnomes.

It doesn't matter whether you're new to crochet or whether you've been doing it for years - thanks to the thorough explanation of the basics (at the end of the book, along with a glossary of the abbreviations used in the instructions) and the clearly structured patterns, anyone can create a festive home for their gnomes.

The carefully selected colors and the small amounts of materials required make the projects in this book ideal for whiling away an enjoyable evening of crochet. Take inspiration from my ideas and brighten up your home with the magic of Christmas!

So, are you ready to get started on some crochet? It's bound to get you in the mood for the festive season. In fact, by the time you've finished your first gnome, you'll almost be able to smell the cinnamon! Sounds irresistible, doesn't it? There's no time like the present—let's pick up those crochet hooks!

Have fun!

POST

THE GNOMES ARE MOVING IN!

A WINTER WONDERLAND

WARM AND COZY

TASTY TREATS

THE GNOMES ARE MOVING IN!

We've all heard of Christmas elves. But did you know there were Christmas gnomes, too? It's true! Every year, gnomes set out from the North Pole to spend the festive season with humans. They write little notes and get up to all kinds of practical jokes – and they suddenly become invisible any time someone is near. Just like any other living creatures, not all gnomes look alike. Some cover up with hats, some let their hair hang down in braids; some wear pants, others wear dresses; then there are those who have big bushy beards. Every gnome is unique!

This section will teach you how to create your very own gnomes. Enjoy!

Frida and Lars

Gnomes with dangling legs

The tradition of Christmas gnomes originates in Scandinavia, and so they generally tend to have Nordic names.

Also known as *nisse* or *tomte*, the gnomes often go by Swedish or Danish names like Lars, Erik, or Alvi. Other nice names for gnomes include Ida, Frida, Elvin, Fredi, or Brikka.

DIFFICULTY: 2

HEIGHTS

Frida: 11.5 cm (about 4.5")
Lars: 16.5 cm (about 6.5")
Hat: 6.5 cm (about 2.6")

MATERIAL

- Knit Picks Animation (125 m, 50 g) in White (#N2702), Fiesta Red (#N2686), Clementine (#N2681), Blush (#N2677), Jalapeño (#N2690), 1 skein; Swan (#N2700), Blue (#N2676), and Jade (#N2689), scraps
- 2.75 mm crochet hook (U.S size C-2)
- Tapestry needle
- Craft glue
- Stuffing (e.g., fiberfill)
- Blush

Stripe sequence

Alternate between 1 rnd in Swan and 1 rnd in Jalapeño.

Color changes

On the last st of one MC, stop when you have two loops on your hook. Yarn over with the new MC and pull through both loops on the hook to create a precise color transition.

Pattern

With the exception of the scarf, crochet all sections in spiral rounds. Mark the start of each round with a stitch marker or yarn of a contrasting color.

FRIDA

Head and body

Make a magic circle in Blush. (See page 98 for explanations of how to do this and various other crochet techniques, as well as a list of all the abbreviations used in this book.)

Rnd 1: Work 6 sc into circle (= 6 st).

Continue to work in spiral rnd.

Rnd 2: Work 2 sc in each sc (= 12 st).

Rnd 3: Work 2 sc in every second sc (= 18 st).

Rnd 4: Work 2 sc in every third sc (= 24 st).

Rnd 5: Work 2 sc in every fourth sc (= 30 st).

Rnds 6–7: Work 30 sc.

Rnd 8: *Sc in next 3 sts, sc2tog; rep from *around (= 24 st).

Rnd 9: Work 24 sc.

Rnd 10: *Sc in next 2 sts, sc2tog; rep from * around (= 18 st).

Rnd 11: *Sc in next st, sc2tog; rep from * around (= 12 st).

Fill the head with stuffing, distributing it evenly to ensure there are no lumps.

Rnd 12 (White): Work 12 sc into back loops.

Rnd 13: Work 2 sc in every second sc (= 18 st).

Rnds 14–19: Work 18 sc.

Rnd 20: *Sc in next st, sc2tog; rep from * around (= 12 st).

Fill the body with stuffing.

Rnd 21: Sc2tog around (= 6 st).

To fasten off, cut off the yarn leaving a long tail, pull it through the final loop, thread it through a needle, and weave it into the last 6 st.

Leg (2x)

Make a magic circle in Blush.

Rnd 1: Work 6 sc into circle (= 6 st).

Continue to work in spiral rnd.

Rnd 2: Work 6 sc.

Rnd 3: Work 2 sc in every second sc (= 9 st).

Rnds 4–5: Work 9 sc.

Rnd 6: *Sc in next st, sc2tog; rep from * around (= 6 st).

To fasten off, cut off the yarn leaving a long tail, pull it through the final loop, thread it through a needle, and weave it into the last 6 st.

From the foot, work 8 ch in Blush to create a leg. Cut off the yarn and weave it in to join the leg to the body.

Repeat the process to make the second leg.

Arm (2x)

Make a magic circle in Blush.
Rnd 1: Work 6 sc into circle (= 6 st).
Continue to work in spiral rnd.
Rnds 2–3: Work 6 sc.
To fasten off, cut off the yarn leaving a long tail, pull it through the final loop, thread it through a needle, and weave into the last 6 st. From the hand, work 6 ch in Blush to create an arm. Cut off the yarn and weave it in to join the arm to the body.

Dress

Crochet the dress onto the body. Do this with the head pointing toward you. Draw up a new loop of Clementine through a front loop at Rnd 11 of the body.
Rnd 1: Work 12 sc into front loops of Rnd 11 of body (= 12 st).
Continue to work in spiral rnd.
Rnd 2: Work 2 sc in every second sc (= 18 st).
Rnd 3: Work 2 sc in every third sc (= 24 st).
Rnds 4–7: Work 24 sc.
Rnds 8–10 (Fiesta Red): Work 24 sc.
Rnd 11: Work 2 sc in every fourth sc (= 30 st).

Rnd 12: Work 30 sc.
Rnd 13 (White): * 1 sc, 1 ch; rep from * around.
Close with 1 sl st. Cut the yarn and weave in.

Hair

Make a magic circle in White.
Rnd 1: Work 6 sc into circle (= 6 st).
Continue to work in spiral rnd.
Rnd 2: Work 2 sc in each sc (= 12 st).
Rnd 3: Work 2 sc in every second sc (= 18 st).
Rnd 4: Work 2 sc in every third sc (= 24 st).
Rnd 5: Work 2 sc in every fourth sc (= 30 st).
Rnds 6–9: Work 30 sc.
Rnd 10: 4 sc, 1 hdc, 8 dc, 1 hdc, 2 sc, 1 sl st, 2 sc, 3 hdc, 8 sc.
Close with 1 sl st. Cut the yarn and weave in.

Bun

Make a magic circle in White.
Rnd 1: Work 6 sc into circle (= 6 st).
Continue to work in spiral rnd.
Rnd 2: Work 2 sc in each sc (= 12 st).
Rnd 3: Work 2 sc in every second sc (= 18 st).
Rnds 4–5: Work 18 sc.
Rnd 6: *Sc in next 2 sts, sc2tog; rep from * around (= 12 st).
Close with 1 sl st. Cut the yarn and weave in.

Ribbon

Make a magic circle in Fiesta Red, but do not tighten it yet.
Rnd 1: Work into circle as follows: 3 ch, 2 dc, 3 ch, 1 sl st into circle; 3 ch, 2 dc, 3 ch, 1 sl st into circle; * 5 ch; starting in second ch from hook, 4 sl st onto ch st, 1 sl st into circle; rep 1x from * around. Now tighten magic circle.
Cut the yarn and weave in.

Scarf

Ch 50 in Fiesta Red. Continue to work in rows.

Row 1: Starting in third ch from hk, work 48 hdc (= 48 st). Turn with 2 ch at end of row.

Row 2: Work 48 hdc.

Cut the yarn and weave in.

Hat

Ch 31 in Fiesta Red and close circle with 1 sl st.

Continue to work in spiral rnd.

Rnd 1: Work 30 sc (= 30 st).

Rnds 2–6: Work 30 sc.

Rnd 7: *Sc in next 3 sts, sc2tog; rep from * around (= 24 st).

Rnds 8–9: Work 24 sc.

Rnd 10: *Sc in next 2 sts, sc2tog; rep from * around (= 18 st).

Rnds 11–12: Work 18 sc.

Rnd 13: *Sc in next st, sc2tog; rep from * around (= 12 st).

Rnds 14–17: Work 12 sc.

Rnd 18: *Sc in next st, sc2tog; rep from * around (= 8 st).

Rnd 19: Work 8 sc.

Rnd 20: Sc2tog around (= 4 st).

To fasten off, cut off the yarn leaving a long tail, pull it through the final loop, thread it through a needle, and weave it into the last 4 st.

Crochet a border in White at Rnd 1 of the hat. Do this with the top of the hat pointing toward you.

Rnd 1: * 1 sc, 1 ch; rep from * around (= 60 st). Close with 1 sl st.

Cut the yarn and weave in.

Finishing off

For the face, stitch on a nose in Blush over 2 st. To the left and right of it, stitch on the eyes in Blue and White. Finally, dab some blush onto the cheeks.

Glue the hair onto the head. Fill the bun with stuffing and glue it onto the hair. Wind Fiesta Red yarn 3x around the bun and glue the yarn to the bun.

Glue on the scarf as well. Sew or glue the hat onto the head, and push it down a little as well so that it is not standing up perfectly straight. Fasten off all yarn.

LARS

To crochet the head, body, arms, and legs, follow the same procedure as for Frida.

Shirt and pants

Draw up a new loop of Jade through a front loop at Rnd 11 of the body. Do this with the head pointing toward you.

Rnd 1: Work 12 sc into front loops of Rnd 11 of body (= 12 st).

Continue to work in spiral rnd.

Rnd 2 (Swan): Work 2 sc in every second sc (= 18 st).

Rnd 3 (Jade): Work 2 sc in every third sc (= 24 st).

Rnds 4–7: Follow the stripe sequence on page 14 and work 24 sc in each color.

Rnd 8 (Jalapeño): Work 24 sc into back loops.

Rnds 9–11: Work 24 sc.

Rnd 12: Work as follows for the first pant leg: 12 sc, 3 ch, skip 12 st. Close with 1 sl st (= 15 st).

Rnd 13: 12 sc, 3 sc into ch st.

Rnd 14: Work 15 sc. Close with 1 sl st.

Cut the yarn and weave in.

Work the second pant leg into skipped 12 st from Rnd 12. Do this with the head pointing toward you.

Rnd 12 (second pant leg): 12 sc, 3 sc into ch st of first pant leg. Close with 1 sl st (= 15 st).

Rnd 13–14: Work 15 sc.

Close with 1 sl st. Cut the yarn and weave in.

Hat and beard

Ch 31 in Fiesta Red and close circle with 1 sl st.

Continue to work in spiral rnd.

Rnd 1: Work 30 sc (= 30 st).

Rnds 2–6: Work 30 sc.

Rnd 7: *Sc in next 3 sts, sc2tog; rep from * around (= 24 st).

Rnds 8–9: Work 24 sc.

Rnd 10: *Sc in next 2 sts, sc2tog; rep from * around (= 18 st).

Rnds 11–12: Work 18 sc.

Rnd 13: *Sc in next st, sc2tog; rep from * around (= 12 st).

Rnds 14–17: Work 12 sc.

Rnd 18: *Sc in next st, sc2tog; rep from * around (= 8 st).

Rnd 19: Work 8 sc.

Rnd 20: Sc2tog around (= 4 st).

To fasten off, cut the yarn leaving a long tail, pull it through the final loop, thread it through a needle, and weave it into the last 4 st.

Draw up a new loop of White on the border (= Rnd 1) of the hat. Do this with the top of the hat pointing toward you.

Rnd 1: Work 30 sc. Close with 1 sl st (= 30 st).

Rnd 2: * 1 sc, 1 ch; rep 17x starting from *; ch 16 (= beard); skip 12 st. Close with 1 sl st. Turn with 1 ch and continue to work beard back into ch st.

Rnd 3: * 5 dc in 1 st; skip 1 ch; 1 sl st into next ch; skip 1 ch; rep 3x starting from *.

Close with 1 sl st into next st of previous rnd. Cut the yarn and weave in.

Finishing off

Sew the arms and legs onto the body. For the face, stitch on a nose in Blush over 2 st. To the left and right of it, stitch on the eyes in Blue and White. Finally, dab some blush onto the cheeks.

Tuck the head into the hat and push the hat down a little so that it is not standing up perfectly straight. Sew or glue it into place, ensuring that the face is framed by the hat and beard. You may need to adjust the beard slightly.

Ida and Nils

Seated gnomes

The long December evenings fly by when the gnomes are around, thanks to their boisterous antics.

Whether it's causing chaos in the kitchen, making footprints in the flour, or leaving cabinet doors open, they're always up to something.

DIFFICULTY: 2

HEIGHTS

Ida: 7 cm (about 2.8")
Nils: 7 cm (about 2.8")
Hat: 6.5 cm (about 2.6")

MATERIAL

- Knit Picks Animation (125 m, 50 g) in White (#N2702), Fiesta Red (#N2686), Clementine (#N2681), Blush (#N2677), Jalapeño (#N2690), Swan (#N2700), and Jade (#N2689), 1 skein; Blue (#N2676), scraps
- 2.75 mm crochet hook (US size C-2)
- Tapestry needle
- Craft glue
- Stuffing (e.g., fiberfill)
- Blush

Stripe sequence

Alternate between 1 rnd in Jade and 1 rnd in Swan.

Color changes

On the last st of one MC, stop when you have two loops on your hook. Yarn over with the new MC and pull through both loops on the hook to create a precise color transition.

Pattern

Work all sections in spiral rounds.
Mark the start of each round with a stitch marker or yarn of a contrasting color.

IDA

Head and body

Make a magic circle in Blush.
Rnd 1: Work 6 sc into circle (= 6 st).
Continue to work in spiral rnd.
Rnd 2: Work 2 sc in each sc (= 12 st).
Rnd 3: Work 2 sc in every second sc (= 18 st).
Rnd 4: Work 2 sc in every third sc (= 24 st).
Rnd 5: Work 2 sc in every fourth sc (= 30 st).
Rnds 6–7: Work 30 sc.
Rnd 8: *Sc in the next 3 sts, sc2tog; rep from * around (= 24 st).
Rnd 9: Work 24 sc.
Rnd 10: *Sc in the next 2 sts, sc2tog; rep from * around (= 18 st).

Rnd 11: *Sc in the next st, sc2tog; rep from * around (= 12 st).
Fill the head with stuffing.
Rnd 12 (Clementine): Work 12 sc.
Rnd 13: Work 2 sc in every second sc (= 18 st).
Rnd 14: Work 2 sc in every third sc (= 24 st).
Rnd 15: Work 24 sc.
Rnd 16: Work 2 sc in every fourth sc (= 30 st).
Rnds 17–18: Work 30 sc.
Rnd 19 (White): Work 30 sc into back loops.
Rnd 20: Work 2 sc in every fifth sc (= 36 st).
Rnds 21–23: Work 36 sc.
Rnd 24: * Sc in the next 4 sts, sc2tog; rep from * around (= 30 st).
Rnd 25: * Sc in the next 3 sts, sc2tog; rep from * around (= 24 st).
Rnd 26: * Sc in the next 2 sts, sc2tog; rep from * around (= 18 st).
Fill the body with stuffing.
Rnd 27: * Sc in the next st, sc2tog; rep from * around (= 12 st).
Rnd 28: Sc2tog around (= 6 st).
To fasten off, cut the yarn leaving a long tail, pull it through the final loop, thread it through a needle, and weave it into the last 6 st.

Skirt

Draw up a new loop of Jalapeño through a front loop at Rnd 18 of the body and crochet around the body as follows.
Rnd 1: Work 2 sc in every fifth sc (= 36 st).
Continue to work in spiral rnd.
Rnd 2 (Jade): Work 2 sc in every sixth sc (= 42 st).
Rnd 3 (Jalapeño): Work 2 sc in every seventh sc (= 48 st).
Rnd 4 (Jade): * 7 dc, 2 dc in 1 st; rep 5x starting from * (= 54 st).
Rnd 5 (Jalapeño): * 5 dc in 1 st; skip 1 st; 1 sl st; skip 1 st; rep 12x starting from *. End with 5 dc in 1 st; skip 1 st. Close with 1 sl st.
Cut the yarn and weave in.

Arm (2x)

Make a magic circle in Blush.
Rnd 1: Work 6 sc into circle (= 6 st).
Continue to work in spiral rnd.
Rnds 2–4: Work 6 sc.
Rnds 5–11 (Clementine): Work 6 sc.
Fill the arm with stuffing.
Cut the yarn and weave in.
Make the second arm in the same way.

Shoe and leg (2x)

Ch 8 in Fiesta Red.
Row 1: Starting in second ch from hk, work 7 sc (= 7 st).
Continue to work in rows. Turn with 1 ch at end of each row.
Rows 2–4: Work 7 sc.
Continue to work in spiral rnd. Join first and last st of Rnd 4 to create a circle.
Rnd 1: Work 7 sc.

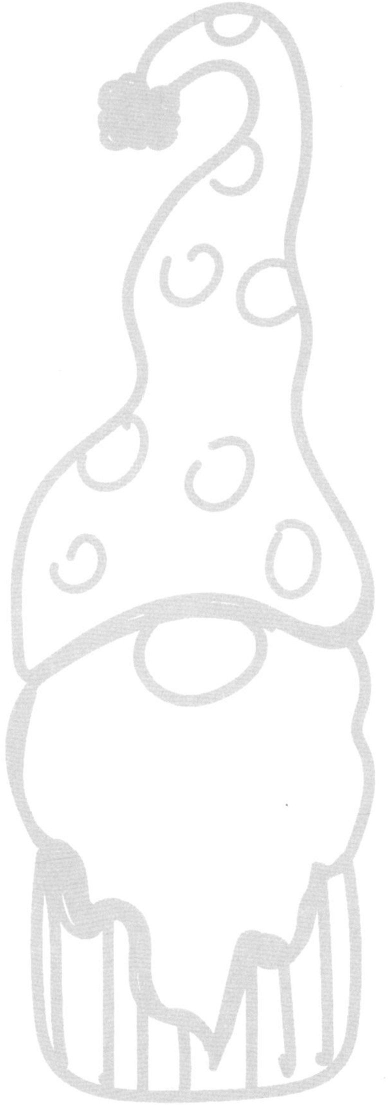

Rnds 2-3: Work 7 sc.
Rnd 4: * 1 sc, sc2tog; rep 1x starting from *; 1 sc (= 5 st).
Rnd 5: Work 5 sc.
Fill the shoe with stuffing, but not completely – leave a little space at the tip of the shoe.
To fasten off, cut the yarn leaving a long tail, pull it through the final loop, thread it through a needle, and weave it into the last 5 st.
For the leg, draw up a new loop of Fiesta Red in an edge st at the top opening and crochet in rnd.
Rnd 1: Work 9 sc (= 9 st).
Rnd 2 (White): Work 9 sc. Close with 1 sl st.
Rnds 3–5: Work 9 sc.
Close with 1 sl st.
Fill the leg with stuffing, distributing it evenly to ensure there are no lumps. Cut the yarn and weave in.
Repeat the process to make the second shoe and leg.

Hair

Make a magic circle in White.
Rnd 1: Crochet 6 sc into circle (= 6 st).
Rnd 2: Work 2 sc in each sc (= 12 st).
Rnd 3: Work 2 sc in every second sc (= 18 st).
Rnd 4: Work 2 sc in every third sc (= 24 st).
Rnd 5: Work 2 sc in every fourth sc (= 30 st).
Rnds 6–9: Work 30 sc.
Rnd 10: 4 sc, 1 hdc, 8 dc, 1 hdc, 2 sc, 1 sl st, 2 sc, 3 hdc, 8 sc (= 30 st).
Close with 1 sl st. Cut the yarn and weave in.

Hat

Ch 31 in Fiesta Red and close circle with 1 sl st.
Rnd 1: Work 30 sc (= 30 st).
Continue to work in spiral rnd.
Rnds 2–6: Work 30 sc.
Rnd 7: *Sc in next 3 sts, sc2tog; rep from * around (= 24 st).
Rnds 8–9: Work 24 sc.
Rnd 10: *Sc in next 2 sts, sc2tog; rep from * around (= 18 st).
Rnds 11–12: Work 18 sc.
Rnd 13: *Sc in next st, sc2tog; rep from * around (= 12 st).
Rnds 14–17: Work 12 sc.
Rnd 18: *Sc in next st, sc2tog; rep from * around (= 8 st).
Rnd 19: Work 8 sc.
Rnd 20: Sc2tog around (= 4 st).
To fasten off, cut the yarn leaving a long tail, pull it through the final loop, thread it through a needle, and weave it into the last 4 st.
Crochet a border in White at Rnd 1 of the hat. Do this with the top of the hat pointing toward you.
Rnd 1: * 1 sc, 1 ch; rep from * around. Close with 1 sl st (= 60 st).
Cut yarn and weave in.

Finishing off

Glue the hair onto the head. For the braids, cut 2x 6 strands of yarn approximately 8 cm (about 3.1") long. Interlace the threads in halves, tie them into Rnd 11 of the hair and braid the strands. Secure with a ribbon in Fiesta Red. Sew or glue the hat onto the head, and push it down a little as well so that it is not standing up perfectly straight. Sew on the arms between Rnds 12 and 13 of the body. Sew the legs onto the body with whip stitches in such a way that your gnome can sit up without falling over. Close the open seam at the heel. For the face, stitch on a nose in Blush over 2 st. To the left and right of it, stitch on the eyes in Blue and White. Finally, dab some blush onto the cheeks. Fasten off all yarn.

NILS

Head and body

Make a magic circle in Blush.

Rnd 1: Work 6 sc into circle (= 6 st).
Rnd 2: Work 2 sc in each sc (= 12 st).
Rnd 3: Work 2 sc in every second sc (= 18 st).
Rnd 4: Work 2 sc in every third sc (= 24 st).
Rnd 5: Work 2 sc in every fourth sc (= 30 st).
Rnds 6–7: Work 30 sc.
Rnd 8: *Sc in next 3 sts, sc2tog; rep from * around (= 24 st).
Rnd 9: Work 24 sc.
Rnd 10: *Sc in next 2 sts, sc2tog; rep from * around (= 18 st).
Rnd 11: *Sc in next st, sc2tog; rep from * around (= 12 st).

Fill the head with stuffing, distributing it evenly to ensure there are no lumps.

Rnd 12 (Jade): Work 12 sc.
Rnd 13 (Swan): Work 2 sc in every second sc (= 18 st).

Continue to work following the stripe sequence (see page 22).

Rnd 14: Work 2 sc in every third sc (= 24 st).
Rnd 15: Work 24 sc.
Rnd 16: Work 2 sc in every fourth sc (= 30 st).
Rnds 17–18: Work 30 sc.
Rnd 19 (Jalapeño): Work 30 sc into back loops.
Rnd 20: Work 2 sc in every fifth sc (= 36 st).
Rnds 21–23: Work 36 sc.
Rnd 24: *Sc in next 4 sts, sc2tog; rep from * around (= 30 st).
Rnd 25: *Sc in next 3 sts, sc2tog; rep from * around (= 24 st).

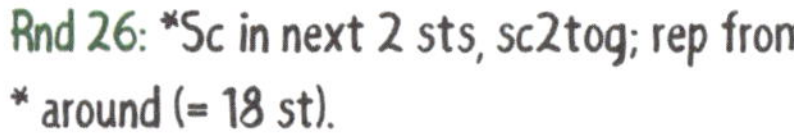

Rnd 26: *Sc in next 2 sts, sc2tog; rep from * around (= 18 st).
Fill the body with stuffing, distributing it evenly to ensure there are no lumps.
Rnd 27: *Sc in next st, sc2tog; rep from * around (= 12 st).
Rnd 28: Sc2tog around (= 6 st).
To fasten off, cut the yarn leaving a long tail, pull it through the final loop, thread it through a needle, and weave it into the last 6 st.

Arm (2x)

Make a magic circle in Blush.
Rnd 1: Work 6 sc into circle (= 6 st).
Rnds 2–4: Work 6 sc.
Rnds 5–11 (Jade): Work 6 sc.
Fill the arm with stuffing, distributing it evenly to ensure there are no lumps.
Cut the yarn and weave it in.
Make the second arm in the same way.

Shoe and leg (2x)

Ch 8 in Fiesta Red.
Row 1: Starting in second ch from hk, work 7 sc (= 7 st).
Continue to work in rows. Turn with 1 ch at end of each row.
Rows 2–4: Work 7 sc.
Continue to work in spiral rnd. Join first and last st of Rnd 4 to create a circle.

Rnd 1: Work 7 sc.
Rnds 2–3: Work 7 sc.
Rnd 4: * 1 sc, sc2tog; rep 1x starting from *; 1 sc (= 5 st).
Rnd 5: Work 5 sc.
Fill the shoe with stuffing, but not completely – leave a little space at the tip of the shoe.
To fasten off, cut the yarn leaving a long tail, pull it through the final loop, thread it through a needle, and weave it into the last 5 st.

For the leg, draw up a new loop of Fiesta Red in an edge st at the top opening and work in rnd.
Rnd 1: Work 9 sc (= 9 st).
Rnd 2 (Jalapeño): Work 9 sc. Close with 1 sl st.
Rnds 3–5: Work 9 sc. Close with 1 sl st.
Fill the leg with stuffing, distributing it evenly to ensure there are no lumps. Cut the yarn and weave in.

Repeat the process to make the second shoe and leg.

Hat and beard

Ch 31 in Fiesta Red and close circle with 1 sl st.
Rnd 1: Work 30 sc (= 30 st).
Continue to work in spiral rnd.
Rnds 2–6: Work 30 sc.
Rnd 7: *Sc in next 3 sts, sc2tog; rep from * around (= 24 st).
Rnds 8–9: Work 24 sc.
Rnd 10: *Sc in next 2 sts, sc2tog; rep from * around (= 18 st).
Rnds 11–12: Work 18 sc.
Rnd 13: *Sc in next st, sc2tog; rep from * around (= 12 st).
Rnds 14–17: Work 12 sc.
Rnd 18: *Sc in next st, sc2tog; rep from * around (= 8 st).
Rnd 19: Work 8 sc.
Rnd 20: Sc2tog around (= 4 st).
To fasten off, cut the yarn leaving a long tail, pull it through the final loop, thread it through a needle, and weave it into the last 4 st.
Draw up a new loop of White on the border of the hat (= Rnd 1). Do this with the top of the hat pointing toward you.
Rnd 1: Work 30 sc. Close with 1 sl st (= 30 st).
Rnd 2: * 1 sc, 1 ch; rep 17x from * around; ch 16 (= beard); skip 12 st. Close with 1 sl st.
Turn with 1 ch and continue to work the beard back on the ch st.
Rnd 3: * 5 dc in 1 st; skip 1 ch; 1 sl st into next ch; skip 1 ch; rep 3x starting from *. Close with 1 sl st into next st of previous rnd. Cut the yarn and weave in.

Heart

Make a magic circle in Fiesta Red, but do not tighten it yet.
Rnd 1: Work into circle as follows: 3 ch, 2 dc, 1 hdc, 1 sc, 1 ch, 1 sc, 1 ch, 1 sc, 1 hdc, 3 dc, 1 sl st into top ch. Now tighten the magic circle to create a heart shape.
Cut the yarn and weave in.

Finishing off

Sew on the arms between Rnds 12 and 13 of the body. Sew the legs onto the body with whip stitches in such a way that your gnome can sit up without falling over. Close the open seam at the heel. For the face, stitch on a nose in Blush over 2 st. To the left and right of it, stitch on the eyes in Blue and White. Finally, dab some blush onto the cheeks. Tuck the head into the hat and push the hat down a little so that it is not standing up perfectly straight. Sew or glue it into place, ensuring that the face is framed by the hat and beard. You may need to adjust the beard slightly. Glue the heart to the belly. Fasten off all yarn.

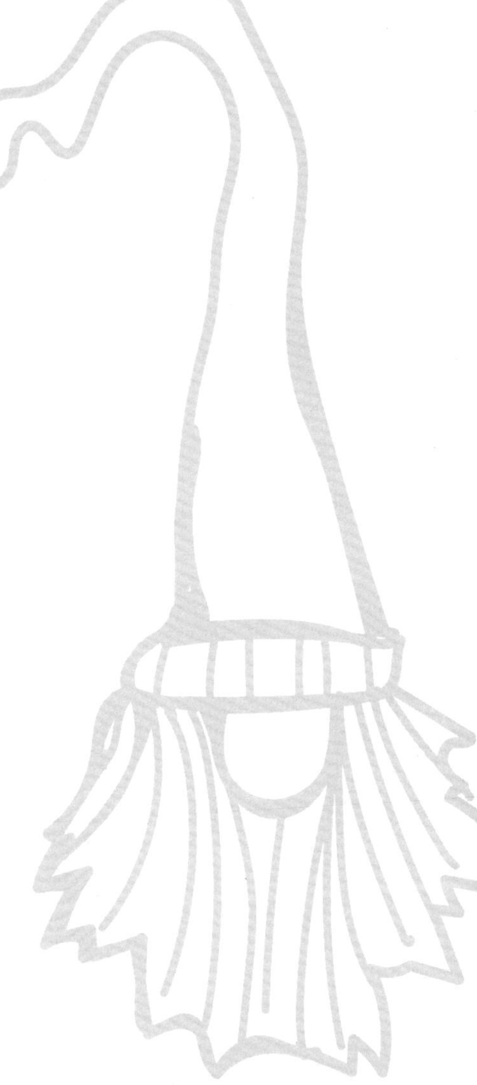

Everything a Gnome Needs

Mittens, shoes, and sack

Gnomes need to wrap up warm for the winter months, and there`s nothing they like more than a cozy handmade sweater. In fact, nothing in their closets is off the rack. Gnomes are industrious creatures, and they make all their own clothing and footwear.

DIFFICULTY

Mittens and sack: 1
Shoes: 3

SIZES

Mittens: 1.5 cm x 1.5 cm (about 0.6" x 0.6")
Sack: 4.5 cm x 5 cm (about 1.8" x 2")
Shoes: 3.5 cm x 1.5 cm (about 1.4" x 0.6")

MATERIAL

- Knit Picks Animation (125 m, 50 g) in Fiesta Red (#N2686), White (#N2702), and Butterscotch (#N2679), 1 skein
- 2.75 mm crochet hook (US size C-2)
- Tapestry needle

Pattern

Crochet the mittens in spiral rounds. Start off the shoes in rows and then continue crocheting in spiral rounds. Mark the start of each round with a stitch marker or yarn of a contrasting color. Crochet the sack in rows.

Mitten (2x)

Make a magic circle in Fiesta Red.

Rnd 1: Work 6 sc into circle (= 6 st).

Continue to work in spiral rnd.

Rnd 2: Work 2 sc in every second sc (= 9 st).

Rnds 3–5: Work 9 sc.

Rnd 6 (White): *Sc in next st, sc2tog; rep from * around (= 6 st).

Close with 1 sl st. Cut the yarn and weave in.

Make the second mitten in the same way.

Crochet a string in Fiesta Red to link up the mittens. To do this, ch 25 and sew the string onto both mittens. Fasten off all yarn.

Shoe (2x)

Ch 8 in Fiesta Red.

Row 1: Starting in second ch from hk, work 7 sc (= 7 st).

Continue to work in rows. Turn with 1 ch at end of each row.

Rows 2–4: Work 7 sc.

Continue to work in spiral rnd. Join first and last st of Rnd 4 to create a circle.

Rnd 1: Work 7 sc.

Rnds 2–3: Work 7 sc.

Rnd 4: * 1 sc, sc2tog; rep 1x starting from *; 1 sc (= 5 st).

Rnd 5: Work 5 sc.

Rnd 6 (White): Work 5 sc.

To fasten off, cut off the thread leaving a long tail, pull it through the final loop, thread it through a needle, and weave it into the last 5 st. Fill the shoe with stuffing, but not completely – leave a little space at the tip of the shoe.

For the leg, draw up a new loop of Fiesta Red in an edge st at the top opening and work in rnd.

Rnd 1: Work 9 sc.

Rnd 2 (White): Work 9 sc.

Close with 1 sl st. Cut the yarn and weave in.

Make the second shoe in the same way.

Close the open seams at the heels of the shoes. Fasten off all yarn.

Sack

Ch 13 in Butterscotch.

Row 1: Starting in second ch from hk, work 12 sc (= 12 st).

Continue to work in rows. Turn with 1 ch at end of each row.

Rows 2–14: Work 12 sc.

You will now have a rectangle. Fold it together and sew up the left and right sides with whip stitches. Then, draw up a new loop at the top edge and crochet a border as follows:

Rnd 1: * 5 dc in 1 st; skip 1 st; 1 sl st; skip 1 st; rep from * around.

Close with 1 sl st. Cut the yarn and weave in.

To make the drawstring for the sack, cut a piece of yarn approximately 20 cm (about 7.9") long in Fiesta Red and the same again in White and twist them together to create a cord. Thread the string through the skipped st at the top edge of the sack and tie it into a bow.

Fasten off all yarn.

A WINTER WONDERLAND

When the brilliant white snow is gleaming in the sunshine and there isn't a cloud in the sky, gnomes can't resist the temptation to go out and play. That means stepping through the front door, which is adorned with a wreath and opens out onto a doormat for wiping off snow-covered shoes. Back home, gnomes live near the forest, which means fir trees are never far away. They also love animals, and so they like to keep the odd birdhouse around to provide nesting places for their feathered friends. Whether they're having snowball fights, building snowmen, or skiing, gnomes know how to have fun.

Come On In!

Front door with wreath and doormat

Some families find that their gnome houseguests start to make themselves at home as early as October. Other gnomes leave things to the last minute and don't move in until December 1.

DIFFICULTY: 2

SIZES

Door: 9.5 cm x 6.5 cm (about 3.7" x 2.6")
Doormat: 4 cm x 8.5 cm (about 1.6" x 3.3")

MATERIAL

- Knit Picks Animation (125 m, 50 g) in Sunbaked (#N2699) and Linen (#N2693), 1 skein; Creme Brulee (#N2683), Mushroom (#N2695), Kenai (#N2691), and Fiesta Red (#N2686), scraps
- 2.75 mm crochet hook (U.S size C-2)
- Tapestry needle
- Strong cardboard
- Craft glue

Pattern

Work all sections in spiral rnd with the exception of the door and the doormat. Mark the start of each round with a stitch marker or yarn of a contrasting color. Crochet the arch at the top of the door in rows starting from a magic circle. This will create a semicircle.

DECORATED DOOR

Door

Make a magic circle in Sunbaked.

Row 1: Work 6 sc into circle (= 6 st).

Continue to work the top arch in rows. Turn with 1 ch at end of each row.

Row 2: Work 2 sc in every second sc (= 9 st).

Row 3: Work 2 sc in every third sc (= 12 st).

Row 4: Work 2 sc in every fourth sc (= 15 st).

Row 5: Work 2 sc in every fifth sc (= 18 st).

Row 6: Work 2 sc in every sixth sc (= 21 st).

Row 7: Work 2 sc in every seventh sc (= 24 st).

Now ch 1 and continue to work in rows along the circumference of the circle as follows:

Row 8: Work 15 sc (= 15 st).

Row 9: Work 15 sc into front loops.

Row 10: Work 15 sc into both loops.

Row 11: Work 15 sc into front loops.

Rows 12–21: Rep rows 10 and 11.

Row 22: Work 15 sc into both loops.

Don`t turn! Continue to work around the door with sc in Creme Brulee as follows: 1 ch, 14 sc, 24 sc around the arch, 14 sc, 1 ch, 15 sc. Close with 1 sl st.

Cut the yarn and weave in.

Doorknob

Make a magic circle in Mushroom.

Rnd 1: Work 8 sc into circle (= 8 st).

Continue to work in spiral rnd.

Rnd 2: Work 8 sc.

Close with 1 sl st. Cut the yarn and weave in.

Wreath

Make a magic circle in Kenai.

Rnd 1: Work 18 sc into circle (= 18 st).

Continue to work in spiral rnd.

Rnd 2: Crochet into back loops: * 3 ch, 2 sl st into second ch from hk, 1 sl st into next ch, 1 sl st into next sc of Rnd 1; rep 17x starting from *. Close with 1 sl st.

Now crochet into front loops of Rnd 1: * 3 ch, 2 sl st into second ch from hk, 1 sl st into next ch, 1 sl st into next sc of Rnd 1; rep. 17x starting from *.

Close with 1 sl st. Cut off thread and pull through.

Ribbon

Make a magic circle in Fiesta Red, but do not tighten it yet.

Rnd 1: Work into circle as follows: 3 ch, 2 dc, 3 ch, 1 sl st into circle; 3 ch, 2 dc, 3 ch, 1 sl st into ring; * 5 ch; starting in second ch from hk, 4 sl st onto ch st, 1 sl st into circle; rep 1x from * around.

Tighten magic circle. Cut the yarn and weave in.

DOORMAT

Ch 21 in Linen.

Row 1: Starting in second ch from hk, work 20 sc (= 20 st).

Continue to work in rows. Turn with 1 ch at end of each row.

Rnd 2: * 1 sc, 1 SP-2 (see page 98); rep starting from *.

Rnd 3: * 1 SP-2; 1 sc, rep starting from * around.

Rnds 4-12: Rep Rnds 2 and 3.

Draw up a new loop of Kenai at Row 1 and at Row 12 and work 20 sl st in each loop.

Finishing off

Fasten off all yarn. If you want to make the door and doormat a little more stable, you can glue them to some cardboard. Glue the ribbon onto the wreath and the wreath and doorknob onto the door. Embroider two stylized fir trees onto the doormat in Kenai.

Special Delivery, Gnome Style

Mailbox

Santa Claus is not the only one who gets a lot of mail in the run-up to Christmas. Gnomes communicate with humans by writing little notes. They use these to ask for favors or tell stories about their many adventures.

DIFFICULTY: 2

SIZE

3.5 cm x 4.5 cm (about 1.4" x 1.8")

MATERIAL

- Knit Picks Animation (125 m, 50 g) in Fiesta Red (#N2686) and White (#N2702), 1 skein
- 2.75 mm crochet hook (U.S size C-2)
- Tapestry needle

POST

Pattern

Crochet the lid and base in rows. Work the sides of the box in spiral rounds. Mark the start of each round with a stitch marker or yarn of a contrasting color.

Lid

Ch 11 in White.
Row 1: Starting in second ch from hk, work 10 sc (= 10 st).
Continue to work in rows. Turn with 1 ch at end of each row.
Rows 2–3: Work 10 sc.
Continue to work around the lid.
Rnd 1: 1 ch, 1 sc, [1 sc, 1 ch, 1 sc] in 1 st (= first corner), 8 sc, [1 sc, 1 ch, 1 sc] in 1 st (= second corner), 1 sc, [1 sc, 1 ch, 1 sc] in 1 st (= third corner), 8 sc, 1 sl st into first st (= fourth corner) (= 29 st).
Rnd 2: 1 ch, 3 sc, * 4 ch; starting in second ch from hk, 3 sl st onto ch st; 2 sc into previous rnd, 3 ch; starting in second ch from hk, 2 sl st onto ch st; 2 sc into previous rnd; rep 1x starting from *; 4 ch; starting in second ch from hk, 3 sl st onto ch st; 5 sc into previous rnd; close with 1 sl st (= 17 st).
Cut the yarn and weave in.

Box

Ch 11 in Fiesta Red to make the base.
Row 1: Starting in second ch from hk, work 10 sc (= 10 st).
Continue to work in rows. Turn with 1 ch at end of each row.
Rows 2–3: Work 10 sc.
Continue to work base in spiral rnd.
Rnd 1: 1 ch, 1 sc, [1 sc, 1 ch, 1 sc] in 1 st (= first corner), 8 sc, [1 sc, 1 ch, 1 sc] in 1 st (= second corner), 1 sc, [1 sc, 1 ch, 1 sc] in 1 st (= third corner), 8 sc, 1 sl st into first st (= fourth corner) (= 29 st).
Rnd 2: Work 29 sc into back loops.
Rnds 3–11: Work 29 sc.
Close with 1 sl st. Cut the yarn and weave in.

Finishing off

Embroider the word "Post" onto the box in White. Then, sew the lid onto the fourth side of the box with whip stitches so that it can be opened. Fasten off all yarn.

WHAT MIGHT THE GNOMES WRITE? HERE ARE SOME SUGGESTIONS

HELLO!

Thank you for the delicious cookies. They were amazing! It's gone very cold outside and the first snow is falling. How about a snowball fight? I love snow, which is good because there's so much of it up at the North Pole with Santa. I can't wait for all the fun we're going to have tomorrow!
Yours gnomishly,
Lars, your Christmas gnome

HELLO!

I love Christmas cookies. Unfortunately, I just have so much to do right now, and I don't have time to make any myself. Do you think you could bake some for me? I've provided all the ingredients. Thank you so much!
Yours gnomishly,
Lars, your Christmas gnome

HELLO!

I'm sure you're wondering why a little door has appeared all of a sudden.
My name is Lars and I'm a Christmas gnome. I work with Santa Claus. Every year at Christmastime, Santa's elves send us out to add a little fun and mischief to the festive season for families all over the world. I would love to spend this Christmas in your home – but only if it's OK with you, of course!

I'll spend the daytime in bed on the other side of my front door, getting some well-earned rest. But at night, when you're all fast asleep, I'll work on Christmas gifts, bake cookies, and help Santa with all the preparations for the big day. You mustn't see me, though, or I'll lose my magical powers. That's a shame, because I'd love to meet you in person, but you can write me little notes and put them in my mailbox. I'll be sure to write back. By the way, I absolutely love cookies, so if you could leave a couple outside my door to keep my strength up, it would make my day. It will help me to work even harder! I can't wait to spend Christmas with you.
Yours gnomishly,
Lars, your Christmas gnome

Playing in the Snow

Snowman and snowballs

Gnomes love snow! Every Christmas, they hold a snowman-building contest. All the gnomes try to build the most impressive snowmen they can, and the best one wins! After that, things tend to get a little chaotic as the gnomes all get together to finish off the event with an enormous snowball fight.

DIFFICULTY: 1

SIZES

Snowman: 8 cm (about 3.1")
Snowball: 1.5 cm (about 0.6") in diameter

MATERIAL

- Knit Picks Animation (125 m, 50 g) in White (#N2702) and Azure (#N2674), 1 skein; Black (#N2675) and Clementine (#N2681), scraps
- 2.75 mm crochet hook (U.S size C-2)
- Tapestry needle
- Strong cardboard
- Craft glue
- Stuffing (e.g., fiberfill)
- Mini pom-pom maker, 2 cm (about 0.8")

SNOWMAN

Crochet the body and the nose in spiral rounds. Mark the start of each round with a stitch marker or yarn of a contrasting color. Crochet the scarf and hat in rows.

Body

Make a magic circle in White.

Rnd 1: Work 6 sc into circle (= 6 st).

Continue to work in spiral rnd.

Rnd 2: Work 2 sc in each sc (= 12 st).

Rnd 3: Work 2 sc in every second sc (= 18 st).

Rnd 4: Work 2 sc in every third sc (= 24 st).

Rnd 5: Work 24 sc.

Rnd 6: Work 24 sc into back loops.

To help the snowman to stand up straight, cut out a piece of cardboard in a circle with the same diameter as the base of the snowman and glue it to the inside of the base.

Rnds 7–14: Work 24 sc.

Rnd 15: *Sc in next 2 sts, sc2tog; rep from * around (= 18 st).

Rnd 16: Work 18 sc.

Rnd 17: *Sc in next st, sc2tog; rep from * around (= 12 st).

Rnd 18: Work 2 sc in every second sc (= 18 st).

Rnd 19: Work 2 sc in every third sc (= 24 st).

Rnd 20: Work 24 sc.

Rnd 21: Work 2 sc in every fourth sc (= 30 st).

Rnds 22–23: Work 30 sc.

Rnd 24: *Sc in next 3 sts, sc2tog; rep from * around (= 24 st).

Rnd 25: *Sc in next 2 sts, sc2tog; rep from * around (= 18 st).
Fill the body with stuffing, distributing it evenly to ensure there are no lumps.
Rnd 26: *Sc in next st, sc2tog; rep from * around (= 12 st).
Rnd 27: Sc2tog around (= 6 st).
To fasten off, cut off the thread leaving a long tail, pull it through the final loop, thread it through a needle and weave it into the last 6 st.
For the border, draw up a new loop through a front loop at Rnd 5 and crochet around the body as follows:
* 5 dc in 1 st; skip 1 st; 1 sl st; skip 1 st; rep 5x starting from *.
Close with 1 sl st. Cut the yarn and weave in.

Nose

Make a magic circle in Clementine.
Rnd 1: Work 6 sc into circle (= 6 st).
Continue to work in spiral rnd.
Rnds 2–3: Work 6 sc.
Rnd 4: Sc2tog around (= 3 st).
Rnd 5: Work 3 sc.
Cut the yarn and weave in.

Scarf

Ch 50 in Azure. Continue to work in rows. Turn with 2 ch at end of each row.
Row 1: Starting in third ch from hk, work 48 hdc (= 48 st).
Row 2: Work 48 hdc.
Cut the yarn and weave in.

Hat

Ch 9 in Azure. Continue to work in rows.
Row 1: Starting in second ch from hk, work 2 sl st, 6 hdc (= 8 st).
Row 2: 2 ch. Starting in third ch from hk, work 6 hdc, 2 sl st into back loops.
Row 3: 1 ch. Starting in second ch from hk, work 2 sl st, 6 hdc into back loops.
Rep Rnds 2 and 3 until you reach the circumference of the snowman`s head.
Cut the yarn and weave in.

SNOWBALLS

Follow the instructions for the mini pom-pom maker to make as many white snowballs as you like.

Finishing off

Sew the nose onto the face. Join the first and last rows of the hat with whip stitches and join the side with the sl st. Glue the hat onto the head. Use the mini pom-pom maker to make a bobble in Azure and sew it onto the hat. Stitch on the eyes, mouth, and buttons in Black. Fasten the scarf into place on the snowman. Fasten off all yarn.

Fun in the Forest

Fir tree

Gnomes decorate their Christmas trees not with colorful baubles but with apples. After Christmas, they all get together for a big feast with homemade apple pie.

DIFFICULTY: 1

SIZE

6.5 cm x 8.5 cm (about 2.6" x 3.3")

MATERIAL

- Knit Picks Animation (125 m, 50 g) in Kenai (#N2691) and Jade (#N2689), 1 skein
- 2.75 mm crochet hook (US size C-2)
- Tapestry needle
- Strong cardboard
- Craft glue
- Stuffing (e.g., fiberfill)

Pattern

There are two versions of the fir tree that you can make. Crochet the main body of the tree in spiral rounds. Mark the start of each round with a stitch marker or yarn of a contrasting color. Crochet the branches into the front loops of the main body.

Tree

Make a magic circle in Kenai or Jade.
Rnd 1: Work 6 sc into circle (= 6 st).
Continue to work in spiral rnd.
Rnd 2: Work 2 sc in each sc (= 12 st).
Rnd 3: Work 2 sc in every second sc (= 18 st).
Rnd 4: Work 2 sc in every third sc (= 24 st).
Rnd 5: Work 2 sc in every fourth sc (= 30 st).
Rnd 6: Work 2 sc in every fifth sc (= 36 st).
Rnd 7: Work 2 sc in every sixth sc (= 42 st).
Rnd 8: Work 42 sc into back loops.
Rnd 9: Work 42 sc.
Rnd 10: Work 42 sc into back loops.
Rnd 11: Work 42 sc.
To help the tree to stand up straight, cut out a piece of cardboard in a circle with the same diameter as the base of the tree and glue it to the inside of the base.
Rnd 12: *Sc in next 5 sts, sc2tog; rep from * around (= 36 st).
Rnd 13: Work 36 sc into back loops.
Rnd 14: Work 36 sc.
Rnd 15: *Sc in next 4 sts, sc2tog; rep from * around (= 30 st).
Rnd 16: Work 30 sc into back loops.
Rnd 17: Work 30 sc.
Rnd 18: *Sc in next 3 sts, sc2tog; rep from * around (= 24 st).
Rnd 19: Work 24 sc into back loops.
Rnd 20: Work 24 sc.
Rnd 21: *Sc in next 2 sts, sc2tog; rep from * around (= 18 st).
Rnd 22: Work 18 sc into back loops.
Fill the tree with stuffing, distributing it evenly to ensure there are no lumps.
Rnd 23: Work 18 sc.
Rnd 24: *Sc in next st, sc2tog; rep from * around (= 12 st).
Rnd 25: Work 12 sc into back loops.
Rnd 26: Work 12 sc.
Push some more stuffing into the tree.
Rnd 27: Sc2tog around (= 6 st).
Rnd 28: Work 6 sc.
To fasten off, cut off the thread leaving a long tail, pull it through the final loop, thread it through a needle, and weave it into the last 6 st.

Branches

Rotate the tree so that the base is pointing toward you. Draw up a new loop of Kenai or Jade through a front loop at Rnd 7 and crochet around the tree as follows:
* Work [1 sc, 1 hdc, 1 ch, 1 dc, 1 ch, 1 hdc, 1 sc] in 1 st; skip 1 st; 1 sl st; skip 1 st; rep from * until end of rnd. Close with 1 sl st. Cut the yarn and weave in.

Follow the same procedure to crochet more branches into front loops of Rnds 9, 12, 15, 18, 21, and 24.

Finishing off

Fasten off all yarn.

In Tune with Nature

Tree with birdhouse

Gnomes don't much like climbing trees. They're afraid of heights! But they'll do it anyway, because filling up their birdhouse with birdseed or rescuing a cat that's gotten stuck is reason enough to conquer their fears.

DIFFICULTY: 2

SIZES

Tree: 8 cm x 12 cm x 10 cm (about 3.1" x 4.7" x 3.9")
Birdhouse: 3.5 cm (about 1.4")

MATERIAL

- Knit Picks Animation (125 m, 50 g) in Sunbaked (#N2699), 1 skein; Creme Brulee (#N2683), Fiesta Red (#N2686), Mushroom (#N2695), and White (#N2702), scraps
- 2.75 mm crochet hook (U.S size C-2)
- Tapestry needle
- Strong cardboard
- Craft glue
- Stuffing (e.g., fiberfill)
- Toothpick

Pattern

Crochet all sections in spiral rounds. Mark the start of each round with a stitch marker or yarn of a contrasting color.

TREE

Trunk

Make a magic circle in Sunbaked.

Rnd 1: Work 6 sc into circle (= 6 st).

Continue to work in spiral rnd.

Rnd 2: Work 2 sc in each sc (= 12 st).

Rnd 3: Work 2 sc in every second sc (= 18 st).

Rnd 4: Work 2 sc in every third sc (= 24 st).

Rnd 5: Work 24 sc into back loops.

Rnds 6–7: Work 24 sc.

To help the tree to stand up straight, cut out a piece of cardboard in a circle with the same diameter as the base of the tree and glue it to the inside of the base.

Rnd 8: *Sc in next st, sc2tog; rep from * around (= 16 st).

Rnds 9-21: Work 16 sc.

Rnd 22: *Sc in next 2 sts, sc2tog; rep from * around (= 12 st).

Rnds 23-27: Work 12 sc.

Fill the tree with stuffing, distributing it evenly to ensure there are no lumps.

Rnd 28: *Sc in next st, sc2tog; rep from * around (= 8 st).

Rnd 29: Work 8 sc.

Add some more stuffing.

Rnd 30: * 1 sc, sc2tog, 1 sc; rep 1x starting from * (= 6 st).

To fasten off, cut off the thread leaving a long tail, pull it through the final loop, thread it through a needle, and weave it into the last 6 st.

Large branch (3x)

Make a magic circle in Sunbaked.

Rnd 1: Work 6 sc into circle (= 6 st).

Continue to work in spiral rnd.

Rnd 2: Work 2 sc in each sc (= 12 st).

Rnd 3: Work 12 sc into back loops (= 12 st).

Rnds 4-6: Work 12 sc (= 12 st).

Fill the branch with stuffing.

Rnd 7: *Sc in next st, sc2tog; rep from * around (= 8 st).

Rnds 8-13: Work 8 sc.

Add some more stuffing.

Rnd 14: * 1 sc, sc2tog, 1 sc; rep 1x starting from * (= 6 st).

To fasten off, cut off the thread leaving a long tail, pull it through the final loop, thread it through a needle, and weave it into the last 6 st. Follow the same procedure to make another two large branches.

Medium-sized branch (3x)

Make a magic circle in Sunbaked.

Rnd 1: Work 6 sc into circle (= 6 st).

Continue to work in spiral rnd.

Rnd 2: Work 2 sc in every second sc (= 9 st).

Rnd 3: Work 9 sc into back loops.

Rnds 4-5: Work 9 sc.

Fill the branch with stuffing.

Rnd 6: *Sc in next st, sc2tog; rep from * around (= 6 st).

Rnds 7-8: Work 6 sc.

Add some more stuffing. To fasten off, cut off the thread leaving a long tail, pull it through the final loop, thread it through a needle, and weave it into the last 6 st. Follow the same procedure to make another two medium-sized branches.

Small branch (3x)

Make a magic circle in Sunbaked.

Rnd 1: Work 6 sc into circle (= 6 st).

Continue to work in spiral rnd.

Rnd 2: Work 6 sc into back loops.

Rnds 3-4: Work 6 sc.

Fill the branch with stuffing, distributing it evenly to ensure there are no lumps. To fasten off, cut off the thread leaving a long tail, pull it through the final loop, thread it through a needle, and weave it into the last 6 st. Follow the same procedure to crochet another two small branches.

Branch stump

Make a magic circle in Creme Brulee.

Rnd 1: Work 6 sc into circle (= 6 st).

Continue to work in spiral rnd.

Rnd 2: Work 2 sc in each sc (= 12 st).
Rnd 3 (Sunbaked): Work 12 sc into back loops.
Rnds 4–6: Work 12 sc.
Fill the branch with stuffing.
Cut the yarn and weave in.

Snow-covered ground

Hold the tree with the top pointing toward you. Draw up a new loop of White through a front loop at Rnd 4 of the trunk.
Rnd 1: Work sc into front loops at Rnd 4 of trunk, working 2 sc in every fourth sc (= 30 st).
Rnd 2: Work into back loops.
Work 2 sc in every fifth sc (= 36 st).
Rnd 3: Work into back loops.
Work 2 sc in every sixth sc (= 42 st).
Rnd 4: Work into back loops.
Work 2 sc in every seventh sc (= 48 st).
Rnd 5: Work into back loops.
Work 2 sc in every eighth sc (= 54 st).
Rnd 6: * 3 ch; starting in second ch from hk, 2 sc, 5 sc into st of previous rnd, 4 ch; starting in second ch from hk, 3 sc, 4 sc into st of previous rnd; rep * around.
Close with 1 sl st.
Cut the yarn and weave in.
Hold the tree with the top pointing toward you. Draw up a new loop of White through a front loop of Rnd 1 of the snow-covered ground and work a decorative seam as follows: * 1 sc, 1 ch; rep from * around. Close with 1 sl st.
Cut the yarn and weave in.

Finishing off

Sew the small branches (with the front loops of Rnd 1) and medium-sized branches (with the front loops of Rnd 2) onto the large branches with whip stitches. Make sure to combine one large, one medium, and one small branch in each case.
Now, use whip stitches to sew the three branch combinations (with the front loops of Rnd 2 of the large branch) to the tree trunk. Then, sew the branch stump with the open end to the trunk using whip stitches. Fasten off all yarn.

BIRDHOUSE

House

Make a magic circle in Fiesta Red.
Rnd 1: Work 5 sc into circle (= 5 st).
Continue to work in spiral rnd.
Rnd 2: Work 2 sc in each sc (= 10 st).
Rnd 3: Work 2 sc in every second sc (= 15 st).
Rnd 4: Work 15 sc into back loops.
Rnds 5–6: Work 15 sc.
Rnd 7: *Sc in next st, sc2tog; rep from * around (= 10 st).
Fill the box with stuffing.
Rnd 8: Work 10 sc.
Rnd 9: Sc2tog around (= 5 st).
To fasten off, cut off the thread leaving a long tail, pull it through the final loop, thread it through a needle, and weave it into the last 5 st.

Roof

Make a magic circle in Mushroom.
Rnd 1: Work 5 sc into circle (= 5 st).
Continue to work in spiral rnd.
Rnd 2: Work 5 sc.
Rnd 3: Work 2 sc in each sc (= 10 st).
Rnd 4: Work 10 sc.
Rnd 5: Work 2 sc in every second sc (= 15 st).
Rnd 6: Work 15 sc.
Rnd 7: Work 2 sc in every third sc. Close with 1 sl st (= 20 st).
Cut the yarn and weave in.

Finishing off

Use Mushroom yarn to attach a loop to the roof and cross stitch the entrance to the house. Glue the roof to the house. Cut the toothpick to roughly 0.8 cm (about 0.3") and fasten it in place underneath the entrance in such a way that it protrudes approximately 0.4 cm (about 0.2") from the birdhouse. Fasten off all yarn.

Winter Sports

Skis and poles

If there's snow on the ground, there's sure to be a gnome skiing somewhere. In fact, skiing is one of their favorite activities. The little thrill-seekers love hurtling at breakneck speed down snowy slopes, whether it's a small hill or a towering mountain.

DIFFICULTY: 1

SIZE

7 cm x 1.3 cm (about 2.8" x 0.5")

MATERIAL

- Knit Picks Animation (125 m, 50 g) in Bumblebee (#N2678), 1 skein; Mushroom (#N2695), scraps
- 2.75 mm crochet hook (U.S size C-2)
- Tapestry needle
- 2 toothpicks
- Craft glue

Pattern

Work all sections in spiral rounds.
Mark the start of each round with a stitch marker or yarn of a contrasting color.

Ski (2x)

Make a magic circle in Bumblebee.
Rnd 1: Work 4 sc into circle (= 4 st).
Continue to work in spiral rnd.
Rnd 2: Work 2 sc in each sc (= 8 st).
Rnds 3–22: Work 8 sc.
Cut the yarn and weave in.
Follow the same procedure to make the second ski.

Ski pole basket (2x)

Make a magic circle in Mushroom.
Rnd 1: Work 8 sc into circle. Close with 1 sl st (= 8 st).
Cut the yarn and weave in.
Follow the same procedure to make the second basket.

Finishing off

Join Rnd 22 of the skis with whip stitches. Embroider the bindings onto the top sides of the skis in Mushroom (don`t go all the way through to the undersides!). If you like, place the skis crossed over each other and fasten them in place with glue or yarn.
Make the ski poles out of toothpicks. For the grip, wrap Mushroom yarn tightly around roughly 1 cm (about 0.4") of one end of each pole and make a little strap. Fasten everything in place with craft glue. Then, skewer the baskets on the other end of each toothpick and glue them in place around 1 cm (about 0.4") from the tip.

WARM AND COZY

When the weather turns cold and there are storms raging and blizzards whirling outside, gnomes put their feet up and get comfortable on the sofa. Nestled between soft throw pillows and wrapped in blankets, they can recover from the rigors of the day and hatch plans for tomorrow. Since it gets dark early anyway, sometimes a gnome will happily take the opportunity to reach for the knitting needles and craft a new sweater or a nice pair of gloves.

A Gnome's Favorite Spot

Sofa

The sofa is more than just a place for relaxation. Gnomes also like to use it as a springboard to jump around and play, as a venue for impromptu pillow fights, or simply as somewhere to snuggle up with a beloved pet.

DIFFICULTY: 2

SIZE

12 cm x 7 cm x 5.5 cm (about 4.7" x 2.8" x 2.2")

MATERIAL

- Knit Picks Animation (125 m, 50 g) in Jade (#N2689), 1 skein; Linen (#N2693), scraps
- 2.75 mm crochet hook (US size C-2)
- Tapestry needle
- Strong cardboard
- Craft glue
- Stuffing (e.g., fiberfill)

Pattern

Work the legs in spiral rounds. Mark the start of each round with a stitch marker or yarn of a contrasting color. Work all other sections in rows.

Leg (4x)

Make a magic circle in Linen.
Rnd 1: Work 5 sc into circle (= 5 st).
Continue to work in spiral rnd.
Rnd 2: Work 2 sc in each sc (= 10 st).
Rnd 3: Work 10 sc into back loops.
Close with 1 sl st. Cut the yarn and weave in.
Follow the same procedure to crochet another three legs.

Underside of seat cushion

Ch 21 in Jade.
Row 1: Starting in second ch from hk, work 20 sc (= 20 st).
Continue to work in rows. Turn with 1 ch at end of each row.
Rows 2–12: Work 20 sc.
Continue to work around the seat cushion as follows:
Rnd 1: 1 ch, 1 sc (= first corner), 10 sc (= short side), [1 sc, 1 ch, 1 sc] in 1 st (= second corner), 18 sc (= long side), [1 sc, 1 ch, 1 sc] in 1 st (= third corner), 10 sc (= short side), [1 sc, 1 ch, 1 sc] in 1 st (= fourth corner), 18 sc (= long side). 1 sl st into first ch (= 68 st).
Continue to work in spiral rnd.
Rnd 2: Work 68 sc into back loops.
Rnds 3–5: Work 68 sc. Close with 1 sl st. Cut the yarn and weave in.
Cut a piece of cardboard to the size of the underside and glue it to the inside of the underside.

Top of seat cushion

Work the top in Jade, following the same procedure as for Rows 1–12 plus Rnd 1 of the underside.

Back cushion

Ch 26 in Jade.
Row 1: Starting in second ch from hk, work 25 sc (= 25 st).
Rows 2–26: Work 25 sc.
Continue to work around the back cushion as follows:
Rnd 1: 1 ch, 1 sc (= first corner), 23 sc (= short side), [1 sc, 1 ch, 1 sc] in 1 st (= second corner), 25 sc (= long side), [1 sc, 1 ch, 1 sc] in 1 st (= third corner), 23 sc (= short side), [1 sc, 1 ch, 1 sc] in 1 st (= fourth corner), 25 sc (= long side). 1 sl st into first ch (= 108 st).
Cut the yarn and weave in.

Armrest (2x)

Ch 11 in Jade.
Row 1: Starting in second ch from hk, work 10 sc (= 10 st).
Continue to work in rows. Turn with 1 ch at end of each row.

Rows 2–20: Work 10 sc.

Don't turn your work, but make the armrest from here as follows:

Rnd 1: 1 ch, 1 sc (= first corner), 18 sc (= long side), [1 sc, 1 ch, 1 sc] in 1 st (= second corner), 8 sc (= short side), [1 sc, 1 ch, 1 sc] in 1 st (= third corner), 18 sc (= long side), [1 sc, 1 ch, 1 sc] in 1 st (= fourth corner), 8 sc (= short side), 1 sl st into first ch (= 64 st).

Cut the yarn and weave in.

Follow the same procedure to make the second armrest.

Finishing off

Place the top of the seat cushion on top of the underside and join the front loops of both sections with whip stitches. Once three sides are closed up, fill the seat cushion with stuffing, distributing it evenly to ensure there are no lumps, and close the fourth side. Take the square that you have crocheted to make the back cushion and fold it in the center to form a rectangle. Join the three open sides with whip stitches and fill the cushion with stuffing. Take the rectangle for the armrest and fold it in the middle to create a square. Join the three open sides with whip stitches and fill the armrest with stuffing. Finish off the second armrest in the same way. Sew the back cushion to the long side of the seat cushion. Sew the two armrests onto the short sides of the seat cushion and fasten them to the back cushion. Fill the legs with a small amount of stuffing and glue them to all four corners on the underside of the sofa.

Snug as a Bug in a Rug

Blanket and throw pillows

Everyone needs their beauty sleep, and gnomes are no different. Gnomes usually sleep all day so that they have the night free to get important work done, meet up with friends, and have exciting new adventures.

DIFFICULTY: 3

SIZES

Blanket: 6 cm x 6 cm (about 2.4" x 2.4")
Throw pillows: 4 cm (about 1.6") in diameter

MATERIAL

- Knit Picks Animation (125 m, 50 g) in Swan (#N2700), Fiesta Red (#N2686), and Jalapeño (#N2690), 1 skein
- 2.75 mm crochet hook (US size C-2)
- Tapestry needle
- Stuffing (e.g., fiberfill)

Pattern

Work all sections in joined rounds. Mark the start of each round with a stitch marker or yarn of a contrasting color.

BLANKET

Make a magic circle in Fiesta Red.

Rnd 1: Work into circle as follows: 4 ch (= 1 dc, 1 ch), * 1 dc, 1 ch; rep 10x starting from *. Close with 1 sl st (= 24 st).

Rnd 2 (Swan): * 3 dc around next ch, 1 ch; rep 11x starting from *. Close with 1 sl st (= 48 st).

Rnd 3 (Jalapeño): * 3 hdc around next ch, 1 ch, 3 hdc around next ch, 1 ch, [1 hdc, 1 dc, 1 tr, 1 ch, 1 tr, 1 dc, 1 hdc] in 1 st (= corner); rep 3x starting from * (= 60 st). Close with 1 sl st.

Rnd 4: 3 ch (= 1 dc), 11 dc, 1 ch (= first corner), 15 dc, 1 ch (= second corner), 15 dc, 1 ch (= third corner), 15 dc, 1 ch (= fourth corner), 4 dc (= 64 st).

Close with 1 sl st. Cut the yarn and weave in. Fasten off all yarn.

TWO THROW PILLOWS

Circle (4x)

Make a magic circle in Fiesta Red.

Rnd 1: Work into circle as follows: 4 ch (= 1 dc, 1 ch), * 1 dc, 1 ch; rep 7x starting from *. Close with 1 sl st (= 18 st).

Rnd 2 (Swan): * 3 dc around next ch, 1 ch; rep 8x starting from *. Close with 1 sl st (= 36 st). Cut the yarn and weave in.

Follow the same procedure to make another three circles.

Finishing off

For each throw pillow, place one circle section on top of the other, with the left side facing inward. Join the two sections using whip stitches in Jalapeño. Sew through the back loops only. Once you have joined 3/4 of each throw pillow, fill it with stuffing, distributing it evenly to ensure there are no lumps, and then finish joining. Fasten off all yarn.

Comfort Underfoot

Rug and yarn basket

Gnomes like a cozy home, which means plenty of rugs on the floor. Round, square, plain, patterned – they have all kinds. Their favorites are nice fluffy rugs that they can bury their toes in.

DIFFICULTY: 1

SIZES

Rug: 9 cm (about 3.5") in diameter
Yarn basket: 3 cm x 2.5 cm (about 1.2" x 1")

MATERIAL

- Knit Picks Animation (125 m, 50 g) in Fiesta Red (#N2686) and White (#N2702), 1 skein; Bumblebee (#N2678), scraps
- 5–6 miscellaneous scraps of yarn
- 2.75 mm crochet hook (US size C-2)
- Tapestry needle
- Craft glue
- 2 toothpicks and suitable wooden beads (your preference)

Stripe sequence

Alternate between 1 rnd in White and 1 rnd in Fiesta Red.

Color changes

On the last st of one MC, stop when you have two loops on your hook. Yarn over with the new MC and pull through both loops on the hook to create a precise color transition.

Pattern

Crochet all sections in spiral rounds.
Mark the start of each round with a stitch marker or yarn of a contrasting color.

Rug

Make a magic circle in Fiesta Red.
Rnd 1: Work 6 sc into circle (= 6 st).
Continue to work in spiral rnd, pushing through to the back loops in every rnd.
Rnd 2 (White): Work 2 sc in each sc (= 12 st).
Rnd 3 (Fiesta Red): Work 2 sc in every second sc (= 18 st).
Continue to follow stripe sequence.
Rnd 4: Work 2 sc in every third sc (= 24 st).
Rnd 5: Work 2 sc in every fourth sc (= 30 st).
Rnd 6: Work 2 sc in every fifth sc (= 36 st).
Rnd 7: Work 2 sc in every sixth sc (= 42 st).
Rnd 8: Work 2 sc in every seventh sc (= 48 st).
Rnd 9: Work 2 sc in every eighth sc (= 54 st).
Rnd 10: Work 2 sc in every ninth sc (= 60 st).

Rnd 11: Work 2 sc in every tenth sc (= 66 st).
Rnd 12: Work 2 sc in every eleventh sc (= 72 st).
Rnd 13: * 5 dc in 1 st; skip 1 st; 1 sl st; skip 1 st; rep starting from * around.
Close with 1 sl st. Cut the yarn and weave in.

Yarn Basket

Make a magic circle in Bumblebee.
Rnd 1: Work 6 sc into circle (= 6 st).
Continue to work in spiral rnd.
Rnd 2: Work 2 sc in each sc (= 12 st).
Rnd 3: Work 2 sc in every second sc (= 18 st).
Rnd 4: Work 2 sc in every third sc (= 24 st).
Rnd 5: Work 2 sc in every fourth sc (= 30 st).
Rnd 6: Work 30 sc into back loops.
Rnd 7: * 1 sc, 1 SP-2 (see page 98); rep starting from * around.
Rnd 8: * 1 SP-2, 1 sc; rep starting from * around.
Rnds 9–11: Rep Rnd 7 and 8.
Close with 1 sl st. Cut the yarn and weave in.

Finishing off

Fasten off all yarn. Wind scraps of yarn into five or six balls and secure the ends with craft glue. Place the balls into the yarn basket.

TIP If you like, you can make knitting needles out of toothpicks and create a little knitting project. Glue beads to one end of each toothpick so that the tiny work won't slip off the needles.

Time for Dinner!

Table and stools

Gnomes love to knit stripy socks in all kinds of colors, because they get chilled easily and there's nothing worse than cold feet. They also enjoy knitting sweaters and gloves for themselves and their friends.

DIFFICULTY: 1

SIZES

Table: 5.5 cm (diameter) x 3.5 cm (about 2.2" x 1.4")
Stools: 3 cm (diameter) x 2 cm (about 1.2" x 0.8")

MATERIAL

- Knit Picks Animation (125 m, 50 g) in Creme Brulee (#N2683) and Sunbaked (#N2699), 1 skein
- 2.75 mm crochet hook (U.S size C-2)
- Tapestry needle
- Strong cardboard
- Craft glue
- Stuffing (e.g., fiberfill)

Pattern

Crochet all sections in spiral rounds.
Mark the start of each round with a stitch marker or yarn of a contrasting color.

TABLE

Tabletop

Make a magic circle in Creme Brulee.
Rnd 1: Work 6 sc into circle (= 6 st).
Continue to work in spiral rnd.
Rnd 2: Work 2 sc in each sc (= 12 st).
Rnd 3: Work 2 sc in every second sc (= 18 st).
Rnd 4: Work 2 sc in every third sc (= 24 st).
Rnd 5: Work 2 sc in every fourth sc (= 30 st).
Rnd 6: Work 2 sc in every fifth sc (= 36 st).
Rnd 7: Work 2 sc in every sixth sc (= 42 st).
Rnd 8: Work 2 sc in every seventh sc (= 48 st).
Rnd 9 (Sunbaked): Work 48 sc into back loops.
Rnds 10–11: Work 48 sc.
Cut a circle out of cardboard to the diameter of the tabletop and glue it to the inside of the tabletop.
Rnd 12: Work into back loops. *Sc in next 6 sts, sc2tog; rep from * around (= 42 st).
Rnd 13: *Sc in next 5 sts, sc2tog; rep from * around (= 36 st).
Rnd 14: *Sc in next 4 sts, sc2tog; rep from * around (= 30 st).
Rnd 15: Work into back loops. *Sc in next 3 sts, sc2tog; rep from * around (= 24 st).
Rnd 16: *Sc in next 2 sts, sc2tog; rep from * around (= 18 st).
Rnd 17: *Sc in next st, sc2tog; rep from * around (= 12 st).
Fill the tabletop with stuffing, distributing it evenly to ensure there are no lumps.
Rnd 18: Sc2tog around (= 6 st).
To fasten off, cut off the thread leaving a long tail, pull it through the final loop, thread it through a needle, and weave it into the last 6 st.

Table base

Make a magic circle in Sunbaked.
Rnd 1: Work 6 sc into circle (= 6 st).
Continue to work in spiral rnd.
Rnd 2: Work 2 sc in each sc (= 12 st).
Rnd 3: Work 2 sc in every second sc (= 18 st).
Rnd 4: Work 2 sc in every third sc (= 24 st).
Rnd 5: Work 2 sc in every fourth sc (= 30 st).
Rnd 6: Work 30 sc into back loops.
Rnds 7–11: Work 30 sc.
Cut a circle out of cardboard to the diameter of the table base and glue it to the inside of the base. Fill the base with stuffing, distributing it evenly to ensure there are no lumps.
Cut the yarn and weave in.

Finishing off

Sew the base to the front loops at Rnd 14 of the tabletop using whip stitches. Fasten off all yarn.

STOOL (2x)

Make a magic circle in Creme Brulee.

Rnd 1: Work 5 sc into circle (= 5 st).

Continue to work in spiral rnd.

Rnd 2: Work 2 sc in each sc (= 10 st).

Rnd 3: Work 2 sc in every second sc (= 15 st).

Rnd 4: Work 2 sc in every third sc (= 20 st).

Rnd 5 (Sunbaked): Work 20 sc into back loops.

Rnds 6–7: Work 20 sc.

Rnd 8: Work into back loops. *Sc in next 2 sts, sc2tog; rep from * around (= 15 st).

Rnd 9: *Sc in next st, sc2tog; rep from * around (= 10 st).

Fill the stool with stuffing, distributing it evenly to ensure there are no lumps.

Rnd 10: Sc2tog around (= 5 st).

To fasten off, cut off the thread leaving a long tail, pull it through the final loop, thread it through a needle, and weave it into the last 5 st.

Follow the same procedure to crochet the second stool. Fasten off all yarn.

TASTY TREATS

Gnomes have a real sweet tooth! If they're not careful, they can empty a whole cookie jar before anyone else even gets a taste. However, they're also very talented bakers capable of conjuring up all kinds of mouthwatering cookies and cakes.

Sure, they need to clean up all the scattered flour, piles of sugar, and fragments of eggshell, but the results are always worth it. Then, after a successful day of baking, the gnomes can sit back and relax with a restorative mug of hot chocolate.

Let's Get Baking!

Mixing bowl and baking equipment

DIFFICULTY: 2

SIZES

Bowl: 6.5 cm (diameter) x 3 cm (about 2.6" x 1.2")
Spoon: 2.5 cm (diameter) x 6.5 cm (about 1" x 2.6")
Dough ball: 4.5 cm (diameter) x 1.5 cm (about 1.8" x 0.6")
Dough, rolled out: 5.5 cm in diameter (about 2.2")
Rolling pin: 2 cm (diameter) x 10 cm (about 0.8" x 3.9")
Eggshell 1: 2 cm (diameter) x 1.5 cm (about 0.8" x 0.6")
Eggshell 2: 2 cm (diameter) x 2 cm (about 0.8" x 0.8")
Fried egg: 3.5 cm (diameter) x 1 cm (about 1.4" x 0.4")
Whole egg: 2 cm (diameter) x 3.5 cm (about 0.8" x 1.4")
Jars: 3.5 cm (diameter) x 3.5 cm (about 1.4" x 1.4")

MATERIAL

- Knit Picks Animation (125 m, 50 g) in Fiesta Red (#N2686), Swan (#N2700), White (#N2702), Butterscotch (#N2679), Sunbaked (#N2699), Creme Brulee (#N2683), 1 skein; Bumblebee (#N2678); and Azure (#N2674), scraps (optional)
- 2.75 mm crochet hook (US size C-2)
- Tapestry needle
- Craft glue
- Stuffing (e.g., fiberfill)

Pattern

Work all sections in spiral rounds.
Mark the start of each round with a stitch marker or yarn of a contrasting color.

BOWL

Make a magic circle in Fiesta Red.
Rnd 1: Work 6 sc into circle (= 6 st).
Continue to work in spiral rnd.
Rnd 2: Work 2 sc in each sc (= 12 st).
Rnd 3: Work 2 sc in every second sc (= 18 st).
Rnd 4: Work into back loops.
Work 2 sc in every third sc (= 24 st).
Rnd 5: Work 2 sc in every fourth sc (= 30 st).
Rnd 6: Work 2 sc in every fifth sc (= 36 st).
Rnd 7: Work 2 sc in every sixth sc (= 42 st).
Rnd 8: Work 2 sc in every seventh sc (= 48 st).
Rnd 9: Increase every eighth sc (= 54 st).
Rnds 10–15: Work 54 sc.
Rnd 16: Work into back loops.
*Sc in next 7 sts, sc2tog; rep from * around (= 48 st).
Rnds 17–21 (Swan): Work 48 sc.
Rnd 22: *Sc in next 6 sts, sc2tog; rep from * around (= 42 st).
Rnd 23: *Sc in next 5 sts, sc2tog; rep from * around (= 36 st).
Rnd 24: *Sc in next 4 sts, sc2tog; rep from * around (= 30 st).
Rnd 25: *Sc in next 3 sts, sc2tog; rep from * around (= 24 st).
Rnd 26: *Sc in next 2 sts, sc2tog; rep from * around (= 18 st).
Rnd 27: *Sc in next st, sc2tog; rep from * around (= 12 st).
Rnd 28: *Sc in next 2 sts, sc2tog; rep from * around (= 9 st).
To fasten off, cut off the thread leaving a long tail, pull it through the final loop, thread it through a needle, and weave it into the last 9 st.
Tuck all rnds in Swan inward to create a bowl.
Draw up a new loop of Fiesta Red through a front loop of Rnd 3 and crochet a border. Do this with the open side of the bowl pointing toward you.
Rnd 1: Work 18 sl st into front loops of Rnd 3.
Close with 1 sl st.
Cut off thread, pull through, and fasten off.
Embroider snowflakes onto the bowl in White.

SPOON

Make a magic circle in Sunbaked.
Rnd 1: Work 6 sc into circle (= 6 st).
Continue to work in spiral rnd.
Rnd 2: Work 2 sc in each sc (= 12 st).
Rnd 3: Work 2 sc in every second sc (= 18 st).
Rnds 4–6: Work 18 sc.
Rnd 7: *Sc in next st, sc2tog; rep from * around (= 12 st).
Rnds 8–9: Work 12 sc.
Rnd 10: *Sc in next 2 sts, sc2tog; rep from * around (= 9 st).
Rnds 11–20: Work 9 sc (= 9 st).
Fill the handle, and only the handle, with a little stuffing.
Rnd 21: *Sc in next st, sc2tog; rep from * around (= 6 st).
To fasten off, cut off the thread leaving a long tail, pull it through the final loop, thread it through a needle, and weave it into the last 6 st.

DOUGH

Dough in a ball

Make a magic circle in Creme Brulee.
Rnd 1: Work 6 sc into circle (= 6 st).
Continue to work in spiral rnd.
Rnd 2: Work 2 sc in each sc (= 12 st).
Rnd 3: Work 2 sc in every second sc (= 18 st).
Rnd 4: Work 2 sc in every third sc (= 24 st).
Rnd 5: Work 2 sc in every fourth sc (= 30 st).
Rnd 6: Work 2 sc in every fifth sc (= 36 st).
Rnd 7: Work 2 sc in every sixth sc (= 42 st).
Rnds 8–9: Work 42 sc.
Rnd 10: *Sc in next 5 sts, sc2tog; rep from * around (= 36 st).
Rnd 11: *Sc in next 4 sts, sc2tog; rep from * around (= 30 st).
Rnd 12: *Sc in next 3 sts, sc2tog; rep from * around (= 24 st).
Rnd 13: *Sc in next 2 sts, sc2tog; rep from * around (= 18 st).
Rnd 14: *Sc in next st, sc2tog; rep from * around (= 12 st).
Fill the dough with stuffing, distributing it evenly to ensure there are no lumps.
Rnd 15: Sc2tog around (= 6 st).
To fasten off, cut off the thread leaving a long tail, pull it through the final loop, thread it through a needle, and weave it into the last 6 st. Glue the ball of dough into the bowl.

Dough rolled out

Make a magic circle in Butterscotch.
Rnd 1: Work 6 sc into circle (= 6 st).
Continue to work in spiral rnd.
Rnd 2: Work 2 sc in each sc (= 12 st).
Rnd 3: Work 2 sc in every second sc (= 18 st).
Rnd 4: Work 2 sc in every third sc (= 24 st).
Rnd 5: Work 2 sc in every fourth sc (= 30 st).
Rnd 6: Work 2 sc in every fifth sc (= 36 st).
Rnd 7: Work 2 sc in every sixth sc (= 42 st).
Rnd 8: * 3 sc, 3 hdc, 2 dc in 1 st, 3 dc, 3 hdc, 2 sc in 1 st; rep 2x starting from * (= 48 st).
Close with 1 sl st.
Cut off thread, pull through, and fasten off.

ROLLING PIN

Handle (2x)

Make a magic circle in Sunbaked.
Rnd 1: Work 8 sc into circle (= 8 st).
Continue to work in spiral rnd.
Rnds 2–4: Work 8 sc.
Rnd 5: * Sc2tog, 2 sc; rep 1x starting from * (= 6 st).
Rnds 6–7: Work 6 sc. Close with 1 sl st.
Cut off thread, pull through, and fasten off.
Follow the same procedure to make the second handle.

Roller

Make a magic circle in Creme Brulee.
Rnd 1: Work 5 sc into circle (= 5 st).
Continue to work in spiral rnd.
Rnd 2: Work 2 sc in each sc (= 10 st).
Rnd 3: Work 2 sc in every second sc (= 15 st).
Rnd 4: Work 15 sc into back loops.
Rnds 5–19: Work 15 sc.
Rnd 20: Work into back loops: * Sc2tog, 1 sc; rep 4x starting from * (= 10 st).

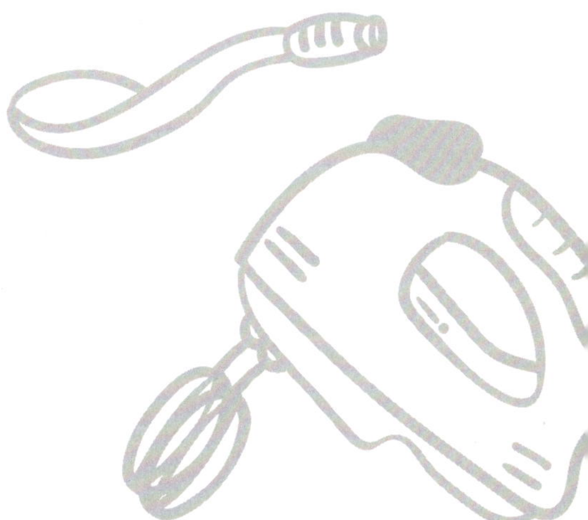

Fill the roller with stuffing, distributing it evenly to ensure there are no lumps.
Rnd 21: Sc2tog around (= 5 st).
To fasten off, cut off the thread leaving a long tail, pull it through the final loop, thread it through a needle, and weave it into the last 5 st. Fill the handles of the rolling pin with stuffing and sew them onto the roller.

EGGS

Eggshell 1 (bottom)

Make a magic circle in Swan.
Rnd 1: Work 6 sc into circle (= 6 st).
Continue to work in spiral rnd.
Rnd 2: Work 2 sc in each sc (= 12 st).
Rnd 3: Work 2 sc in every second sc (= 18 st).
Rnds 4–6: Work 18 sc.
Close with 1 sl st. Cut off thread, pull through, and fasten off.

Eggshell 2 (top)

Make a magic circle in Swan.
Rnd 1: Work 6 sc into circle (= 5 st).
Continue to work in spiral rnd.
Rnd 2: Work 2 sc in each sc (= 10 st).
Rnd 3: Work 10 sc.
Rnd 4: * 1 sc, work 2 sc in next st; rep 3x starting from *; 2 sc (= 14 st).
Rnds 5–6: Work 14 sc.
Close with 1 sl st. Cut off thread, pull through, and fasten off.

Fried egg

Make a magic circle in Bumblebee.
Rnd 1: Work 6 sc into circle (= 6 st).
Continue to work in spiral rnd.
Rnd 2: Work 2 sc in each sc (= 12 st).
Rnd 3: Work 12 sc.
Fill the egg yolk with stuffing.
Rnd 4: Working into back loops, sc2tog around (=6 st).
To fasten off, cut off the thread leaving a long tail, pull it through the final loop, thread it through a needle, and weave it into the last 6 st.
Draw up a new loop of White through a front loop at Rnd 3 of the yolk. Do this with the top of the yolk pointing toward you.
Rnd 1: Work 2 sc in every second sc (= 18 st).
Rnd 2: Work 2 sc in every third sc (= 24 st).
Rnd 3: 3 sc, work 2 sc in next st, 2 hdc, 1 dc, 2 dc in 1 st, 1 hdc, 2 st, work 2 sc in next st, 1 sl st. Leave the remaining sts uncrocheted. Cut off thread, pull through, and fasten off.

Whole egg

Make a magic circle in Swan.
Rnd 1: Work 6 sc into circle (= 6 st). Continue to work in spiral rnd.
Rnd 2: Work 2 sc in each sc (= 12 st).
Rnd 3: Work 2 sc in every second sc (= 18 st).
Rnds 4–6: Work 18 sc.
Rnd 7: * 2 sc, sc2tog; rep 3x starting from *; 2 sc (= 14 st).
Rnds 8–9: Work 14 sc.

Rnd 10: * 1 sc, sc2tog; rep 3x starting from *; 2 sc (= 10 st).
Rnd 11: Work 10 sc.
Fill the egg with stuffing.
Rnd 12: Sc2tog around (= 5 st).
To fasten off, cut off the thread leaving a long tail, pull it through the final loop, thread it through a needle, and weave it into the last 5 st.

FLOUR AND SUGAR JARS

Jar (2x)

Make a magic circle in White.
Rnd 1: Work 6 sc into circle (= 6 st).
Continue to work in spiral rnd.
Rnd 2: Work 2 sc in each sc (= 12 st).
Rnd 3: Work 2 sc in every second sc (= 18 st).
Rnd 4: Work 2 sc in every third sc (= 24 st).
Rnd 5: Work 2 sc in every fourth sc (= 30 st).
Rnd 6: Work 30 sc into back loops.
Rnds 7–15: Work 30 sc.
Close with 1 sl st. Cut off thread, pull through, and fasten off.
Follow the same procedure to make the second jar.

Lid (2x)

Make a magic circle in Sunbaked.
Rnd 1: Work 6 sc into circle (= 6 st).
Continue to work in spiral rnd.
Rnd 2: Work 2 sc in each sc (= 12 st).
Rnd 3: Work 2 sc in every second sc (= 18 st).
Rnd 4: Work 2 sc in every third sc (= 24 st).
Rnd 5: Work 2 sc in every fourth sc (= 30 st).
Rnd 6: Work 2 sc in every fifth sc (= 36 st).
Rnd 7: Work 36 dc into back loops.
Close with 1 sl st. Cut off thread, pull through, and fasten off.
Follow the same procedure to make the second lid in Butterscotch.
Fill the jar with stuffing.

Sew the lids onto the jars using whip stitches. As an option, you can stitch a label onto the jar, such as flour or sugar, using Azure. Fasten off all yarn.

Who Wants Dessert?

Christmas cake

As far as gnomes are concerned, no Christmas is complete without a rich and indulgent cake to share with their friends.

In a gnome household, the Christmas cake tends to get gobbled up almost as soon as it`s out of the oven.

DIFFICULTY: 3

SIZES

Cake: 7 cm (diameter) x 5.5 cm (about 2.8" x 2.2")
Cake slice: 3.5 cm x 5.5 cm (about 1.4" x 2.2")

MATERIAL

- Knit Picks Animation (125 m, 50 g) in Swan (#N2700), Mushroom (#N2695), Fiesta Red (#N2686), Blush (#N2677), and Jalapeño (#N2690), 1 skein
- 2.75 mm crochet hook (US size C-2)
- Tapestry needle
- Strong cardboard
- Craft glue
- Stuffing (e.g., fiberfill)

Pattern

Work the base and top of the cake in rows starting from a magic circle. This will create an open circle. Work the base and top of the cake slice in rows starting from a magic circle. This will create a triangle. Work around both shapes and close into rounds. Then, continue in spiral rounds. Mark the start of each round with a stitch marker or yarn of a contrasting color. For the holly leaves, start with a chain stitch and work around from both sides in joined rounds.

CAKE

Cake base

Make a magic circle in Mushroom.

Row 1: Work 5 sc into circle (= 5 st).

Continue to work in rows. Turn with 1 ch at end of each row.

Row 2: Work 2 sc in each sc (= 10 st).

Row 3: Work 2 sc in every second sc (= 15 st).

Row 4: Work 2 sc in every third sc (= 20 st).

Row 5: Work 2 sc in every fourth sc (= 25 st).

Row 6: Work 2 sc in every fifth sc (= 30 st).

Row 7: Work 2 sc in every sixth sc (= 35 st).

Row 8: Work 2 sc in every seventh sc (= 40 st).

Row 9: Work 2 sc in every eighth sc (= 45 st). Continue to work around the base. Start from the inside of the cake. Don't turn!
Row 10: 1 ch, 18 sc, [1 sc, 1 ch, 1 sc] in 1 st (= first corner), 44 sc, [1 sc, 1 ch, 1 sc] in 1 st (= second corner). Close with 1 sl st (= 68 st). Continue to work in spiral rnd.
Rnd 1: Work 1 ch, 68 sc into back loops.
Rnds 2–3: Work 68 sc.
Rnd 4 (Fiesta Red): Work 68 sc.
Rnd 5 (Swan): Work 68 sc into back loops.
Rnd 6 (Blush): Work 68 sc into back loops.
Rnds 7–10 (Mushroom): Work 68 sc.
Close with 1 sl st. Cut the yarn and weave in. Cut a piece of cardboard to the size and shape of the base and glue it to the inside of the cake base.

Cake Top

Work rows 1–10 in Swan, following the same procedure as for the cake base. Cut off thread 1 m long and pull through.

Assembling the cake

Sew the top onto the base with whip stitches. Make sure that you push through only the back loops on the top, but through both loops on the base. Once you have joined 3/4 of the cake, fill it with stuffing, distributing it evenly to ensure there are no lumps. Then, join the rest of the cake using whip stitches. Fasten off all yarn.

Frosting

Hold the cake with the base pointing toward you.
Draw up a new loop of Swan through a front loop on the top and work the drips of frosting around the edge as follows. Work only on the outside of the cake, not the inside:
Rnd 1: Ch 4; starting in second ch from hk, 1 sl st and 2 sc. 3 sc into Row 10 of cake base.
Ch 5; starting in second ch from hk, 1 sl st and 3 sc. 5 sc into Rnd 10 of cake base.
Ch 3; starting in second ch from hk, 1 sl st and 1 sc. 4 sc into Rnd 10 of cake base.
Ch 5; starting in second ch from hk, 1 sl st and 3 sc. 5 sc into Rnd 10 of cake base.
Ch 4; starting in second ch from hk, 1 sl st and 2 sc; 4 sc into Rnd 10 of cake base.
Ch 5; starting in second ch from hk, 1 sl st and 3 sc; 5 sc into Rnd 10 of cake base.
Ch 3; starting in second ch from hk, 1 sl st and 1 sc. 4 sc into Rnd 10 of cake base.
Ch 5; starting in second ch from hk, 1 sl st and 3 sc. 5 sc into Rnd 10 of cake base.
Ch 4; starting in second ch from hk, 1 sl st and 2 sc; 4 sc into Rnd 10 of cake base.
Ch 5; starting in second ch from hk, 1 sl st and 3 sc. 5 sc into Rnd 10 of cake base.
1 sl st into next st.
Cut the yarn and weave in.

CAKE SLICE

Make a magic circle in Mushroom.
Row 1: Work 1 sc into circle (= 1 st).
Continue to work in rows. Turn with 1 ch at end of each row.
Row 2: Work 2 sc in next st (= 2 st).
Row 3: 1 sc,work 2 sc in next st (= 3 st).
Row 4: 2 sc, work 2 sc in next st (= 4 st).
Row 5: 3 sc, work 2 sc in next st (= 5 st).
Row 6: 4 sc, work 2 sc in next st (= 6 st).
Row 7: 5 sc, work 2 sc in next st (= 7 st).
Row 8: 6 sc, work 2 sc in next st (= 8 st).
Row 9: 7 sc, work 2 sc in next st (= 9 st).
Row 10: 8 sc, work 2 sc in next st (= 10 st).
Continue to work around the base. Start from the inside of the cake. Don't turn!
Row 11: 1 ch, 7 sc, [1 sc, 1 ch, 1 sc] in 1 st (= first corner), 7 sc, [1 sc, 1 ch, 1 sc] in 1 st (= second corner), 7 st, 1 ch. Close with 1 sl st (= third corner) (= 28 st).
Don't turn! Continue to work in spiral rnd.
Rnd 1: Work 1 ch, 28 sc into back loops.
Rnds 2–3: Work 28 sc.
Rnd 4 (Fiesta Red): Work 28 sc.
Rnd 5 (Swan): Work 28 sc into back loops.
Rnd 6 (Blush): Work 28 sc into back loops.
Rnds 7–10 (Mushroom): Work 28 sc.
Close with 1 sl st. Cut the yarn and weave in.
Cut a piece of cardboard to the size and shape of the cake slice and glue it to the inside of the slice.

Top of the cake slice

Work Rows 1–11 in Swan, following the same procedure as for the base of the cake slice. Cut off thread 50 cm long and pull through.

Assembling the cake slice

Sew the top to the base of the cake slice with whip stitches. Make sure that you push through only the back loops on the top, but through both loops on the base of the slice. Once you have joined the two sections of the cake slice, fill the assembled slice with stuffing, distributing it evenly to ensure there are no lumps. Then, close up the last side with whip stitches. Fasten off all yarn.

Frosting

Hold the cake slice with the base pointing toward you. Draw up a new loop of Swan through a front loop on the top and crochet the drips of frosting around the edge as follows. Work only on the outside of the cake, not the inside:
Rnd 1: Ch 5; starting in second ch from hk, 1 sl st and 3 sc. 3 sc into the st of Rnd 10.
Ch 4; starting in second ch from hk, 1 sl st and 2 sc. 2 sc into the st of Rnd 10.
Ch 3; starting in second ch from hk, 1 sl st and 1 sc; 2 sc into st of Rnd 10.
Ch 5; starting in second ch from hk, 1 sl st and 3 sc. 3 sc into Rnd 10.
1 sl st into next st. Cut the yarn and weave in.

Holly leaf (4x)

Ch 10 in Jalapeño.
Rnd 1: Starting in second ch from hk, 2 sc, 1 hdc, 1 dc, 2 dc in 1 st, 1 dc, 1 hdc, 2 sc, 1 ch. Work on back of ch sts: 2 sc, 1 hdc, 1 dc, 2 dc in 1 st, 1 dc, 1 hdc, 2 sc. Close with 1 sl st (= 22 st).
Rnd 2: * Ch 3, 1 sl st into third ch from hk, 3 sl st into st of Rnd 1; starting from *, rep 2x. ** Ch 3, 1 sl st into third ch from hk, 2 sl st into st of Rnd 1; starting from **, rep 1x. *** Ch 3, 1 sl st into third ch from hk, 3 sl st into st of Rnd 1; starting from ***, rep 2x. Close with 1 sl st.
Work 9 sl st above center of holly leaf.
Cut the yarn and weave in.

Berry (4x)

Make a magic circle in Fiesta Red.
Rnd 1: Work 6 sc into circle (= 6 st).
Continue to work in spiral rnd.
Rnd 2: Work 6 sc.
Close with 1 sl st. Cut the yarn and weave in. Follow the same procedure to make another three berries.

Finishing off

Glue the holly leaves onto the cake and the cake slice and then glue the open underside of one berry to each leaf.

Tasty and Warming

Mug of hot chocolate with marshmallows

When gnomes have been up to their usual tricks and going on adventures, they love to sit back on the sofa with a warm mug of hot chocolate, plus a couple of marshmallows for good measure. Hot chocolate tastes even better when it comes after a long walk in the chilly winter air.

DIFFICULTY: 1

SIZE

6 cm (diameter) x 6 cm (about 2.4" x 2.4")

MATERIAL

- Knit Picks Animation (125 m, 50 g) in Fiesta Red (#N2686), Sunbaked (#N2699), Creme Brulee (#N2683), and White (#N2702), 1 skein
- 2.75 mm crochet hook (U.S size C-2)
- Tapestry needle
- Strong cardboard
- Craft glue
- Stuffing (e.g., fiberfill)

Pattern

Work all sections in spiral rounds.
Mark the start of each round with a stitch marker or yarn of a contrasting color.

Stripe sequence

Alternate between 1 rnd in Creme Brulee and 1 rnd in Sunbaked.

Color changes

On the last st of one MC, stop when you have two loops on your hook. Yarn over with the new MC and pull through both loops on the hook to create a precise color transition.

MUG OF HOT CHOCOLATE

Mug

Make a magic circle in Fiesta Red.
Rnd 1: Work 6 sc into circle (= 6 st).
Continue to work in spiral rnd.

Rnd 2: Work 2 sc in every st (= 12 st).
Rnd 3: Work 2 sc in every second sc (= 18 st).
Rnd 4: Work 2 sc in every third sc (= 24 st).
Rnd 5: Work 2 sc in every fourth sc (= 30 st).
Rnd 6: Work 2 sc in every fifth sc (= 36 st).
Rnd 7: Work 36 sc into back loops.
Rnds 8–17: Work 36 sc.
Close with 1 sl st. Cut the yarn and weave in.
Cut a piece of cardboard to the diameter of the base of the mug and glue it to the inside of the mug.

Hot chocolate

Make a magic circle in Sunbaked.
Rnd 1: Work 6 sc into circle (= 6 st).
Continue to follow stripe sequence in spiral rnd.
Rnd 2: Work 2 sc in every st (= 12 st).
Rnd 3: Work 2 sc in every second sc (= 18 st).
Rnd 4: Work 2 sc in every third sc (= 24 st).
Rnd 5: Work 2 sc in every fourth sc (= 30 st).
Rnd 6: Work 2 sc in every fifth sc (= 36 st).
Close with 1 sl st. Cut the yarn and weave in.

Handle

Make a magic circle in Fiesta Red.
Rnd 1: Work 6 sc into circle (= 6 st).
Continue to work in spiral rnd.
Rnd 2: Work 2 sc in every second sc (= 9 st).
Rnds 3–22: Work 9 sc and fill the handle with stuffing.
Close with 1 sl st. Cut the yarn and weave in.

Marshmallow (3x)

Make a magic circle in White.
Rnd 1: Work 6 sc into circle (= 6 st).
Continue to work in spiral rnd.
Rnd 2: Work 2 sc in every second sc (= 9 st).
Rnds 3–4: Work 9 sc.
Close with 1 sl st. Cut the yarn and weave in.
Follow the same procedure to make another two marshmallows and fill all three with stuffing.

Finishing off

Fill the mug with stuffing and sew the hot chocolate to the mug with whip stitches, pushing only through the front loops of Rnd 17 of the mug and both loops of the hot chocolate. Then, draw up a new loop through a back loop at Rnd 17 of the mug, holding the mug with the base pointing toward you. Now crochet 36 sc around the circumference to create a rim. Close with 1 sl st. Cut the yarn and weave in.
Sew the handle to the mug with whip stitches and then sew or glue the marshmallows to the hot chocolate. Finally, embroider snowflakes onto the mug in White. Fasten off all yarn.

Careful, It's Hot!

Pot holders

When the delicious cookies are ready to be taken out of the oven, it goes without saying that the gnomes need pot holders. They don't want to burn their fingers!

DIFFICULTY: 1

SIZES

6 cm x 7.5 cm (about 2.4" x 3")

MATERIAL

- Knit Picks Animation (125 m, 50 g) in White (#N2702) and Fiesta Red (#N2686), 1 skein
- 2.75 mm crochet hook (US size C-2)
- Tapestry needle

Pot holder (2x)

Make a magic circle in Fiesta Red.
Row 1: To make a loop, work 15 sc into circle (= 15 st).
Continue to work in rows. Turn with 1 ch at end of each row.
Row 2: Work 3 sc in 1 st (= 3 st).
Row 3: 1 sc, 3 sc in 1 st, 1 sc (= 5 st).
Row 4: 2 sc, 3 sc in 1 st, 2 sc (= 7 st).
Row 5: 3 sc, 3 sc in 1 st, 3 sc (= 9 st).
Row 6: 4 sc, 3 sc in 1 st, 4 sc (= 11 st).
Row 7: 5 sc, 3 sc in 1 st, 5 sc (= 13 st).
Row 8: 6 sc, 3 sc in 1 st, 6 sc (= 15 st).
Row 9: 7 sc, 3 sc in 1 st, 7 sc (= 17 st).
Row 10: 8 sc, 3 sc in 1 st, 8 sc (= 19 st).
Row 11: 9 sc, 3 sc in 1 st, 9 sc (= 21 st).
Row 12: 10 sc, 3 sc in 1 st, 10 sc (= 23 st).
Crochet around the pot holder, without turning:
1 ch, 10 sc, 15 sc at loop, 10 sc, 1 ch, 23 sc, 1 ch.
Close with 1 sl st. Cut the yarn and weave in.
Follow the same procedure to crochet the second pot holder.

Finishing off

Embroider lines onto the pot holders with long stem stitches in White and Fiesta Red.
Fasten off all yarn.

The Basics

Magic circle

1 Starting from the right, wind the yarn once around your index finger and then once around your thumb on your left hand. Hold the yarn taut between your thumb and index finger.

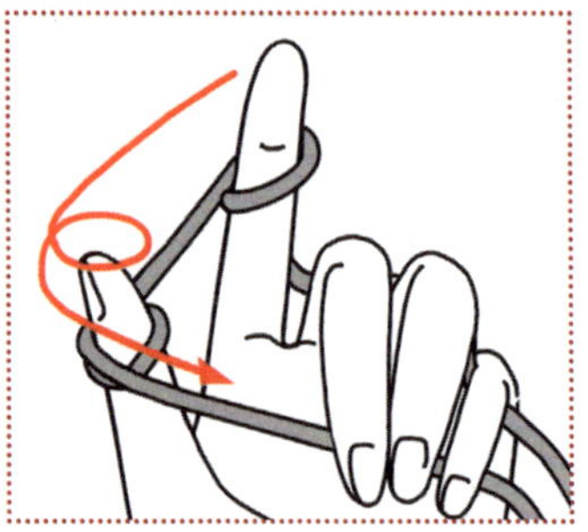

2 Poke your crochet hook under the yarn around your thumb and pull the yarn around your index finger through to form a loop.

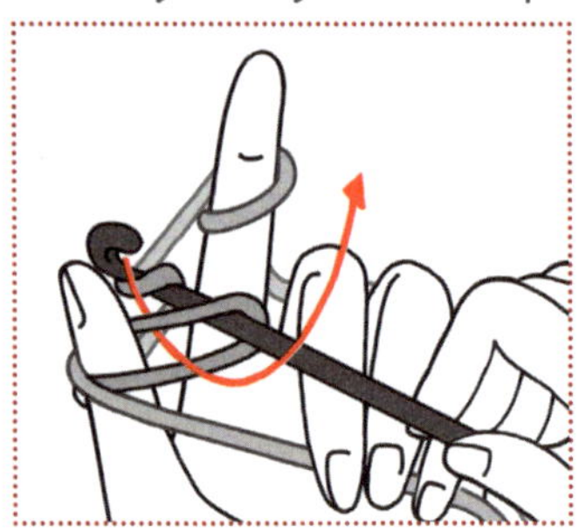

3 Chain one from the loop.

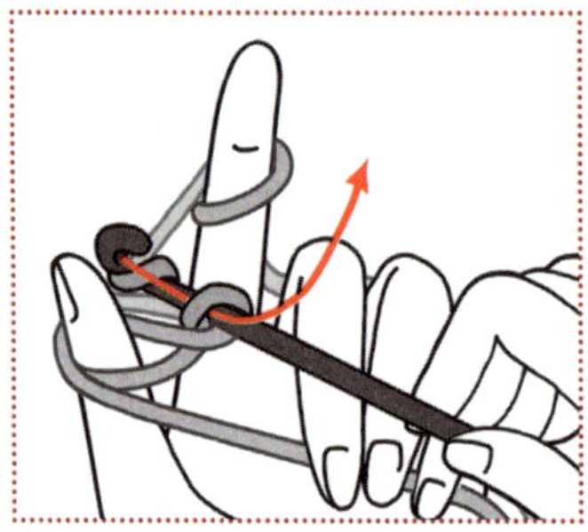

4 To work single crochets into the magic circle, pull the yarn through to form a loop again...

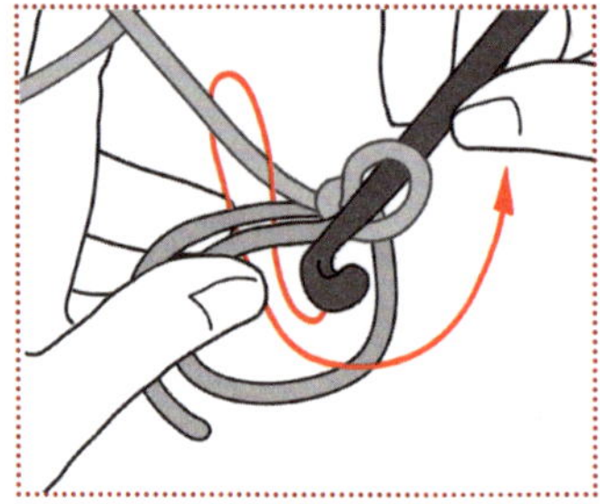

5 ...and create one single crochet out of the two loops. If you're working double crochets into the circle, chain three from the loop and work the required number of double crochets into the circle.

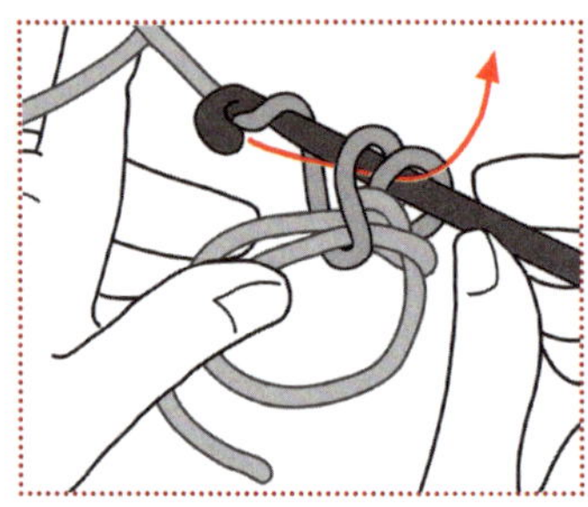

6 Once you've worked the number of stitches, pull on the loose yarn to tighten the circle. Close the magic circle with one slip stitch.

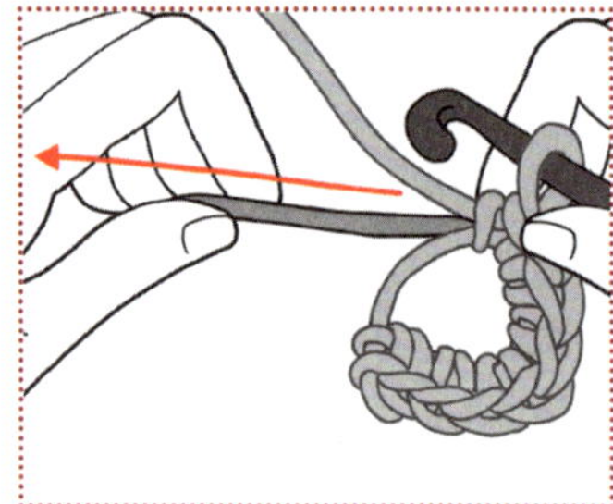

Chain stitch

First, make a starting loop.

1 Hold the yarn between your ring finger and your little finger and route it behind your middle finger. Now guide it around your index finger...

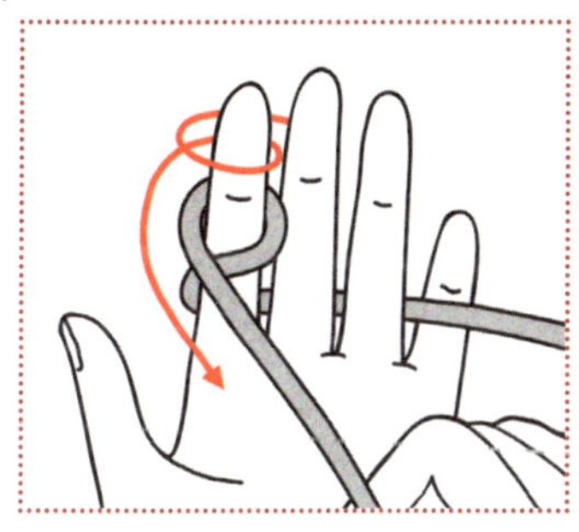

2 ...and loop it around your thumb. The end of the yarn should be sitting in your hand.

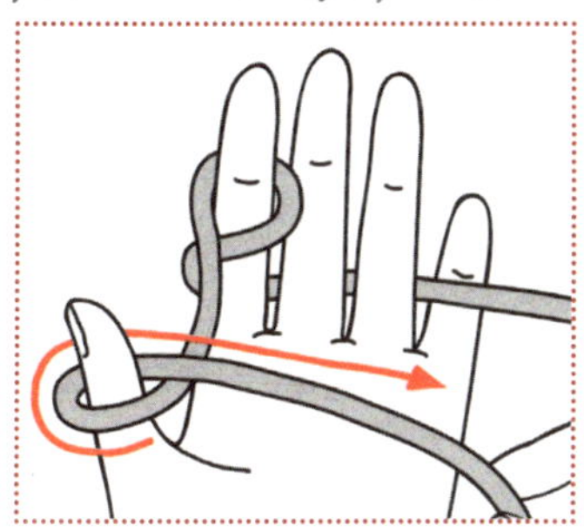

3 Take your hook and pull the yarn from your index finger through the thumb loop. Take your thumb out of the loop.

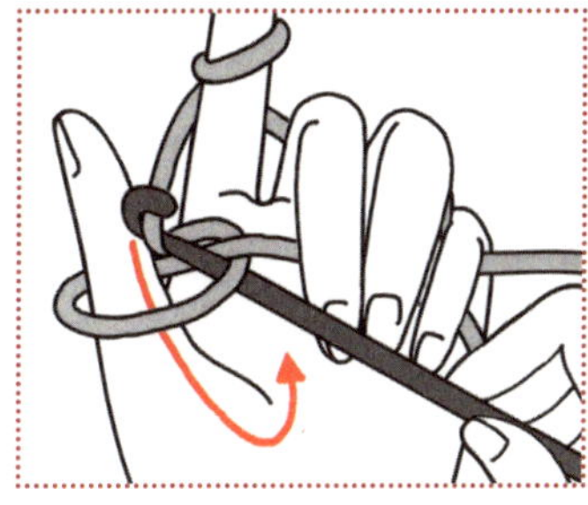

4 Push your thumb under the end of the yarn, which you should be holding in place with your middle, ring, and little fingers.

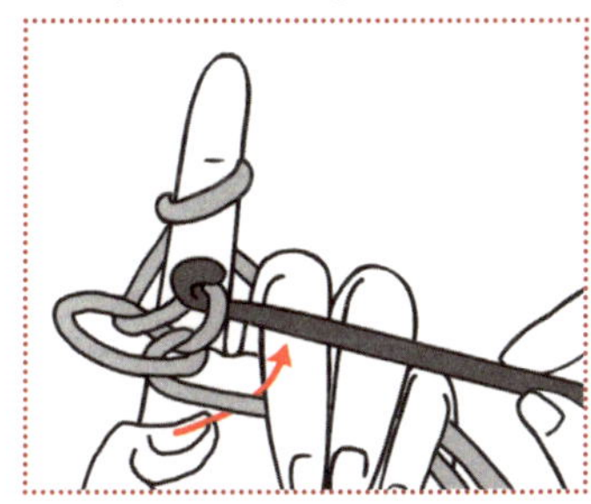

5 Spread your thumb and index finger and pull the starting loop taut on the hook. It should sit on the hook with enough slack to be flexible but not enough that it can slip down.

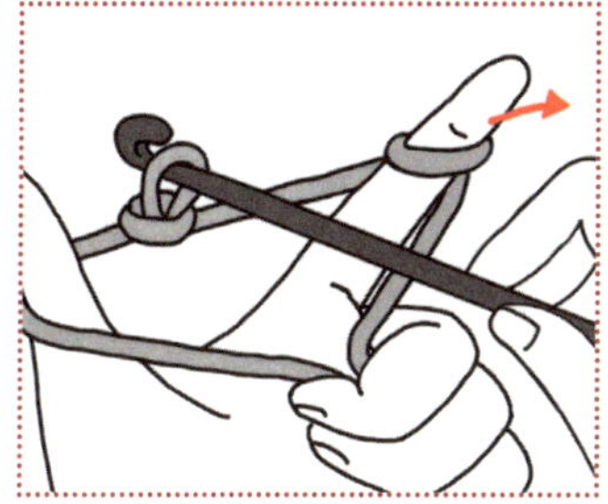

6 To cast on more chains, use the hook to grab the yarn coming from your index finger and pull it through the loop on the hook. That will create a chain stitch.

Single crochet (sc)

1 Push your crochet hook into the second chain from the hook, grab the yarn from behind and pull it forward...

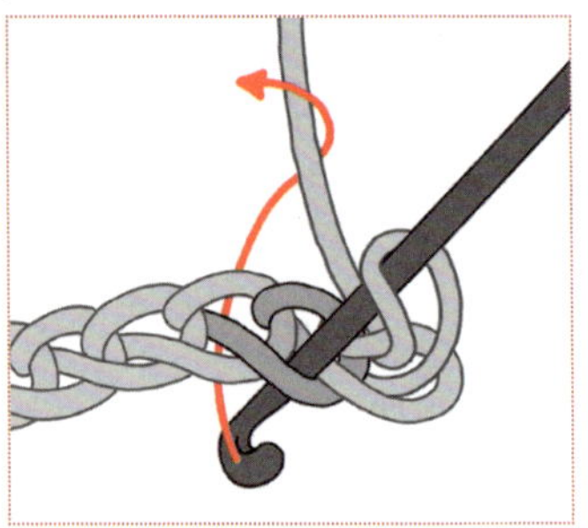

2 ...and through the chain. There should now be two loops on your hook.

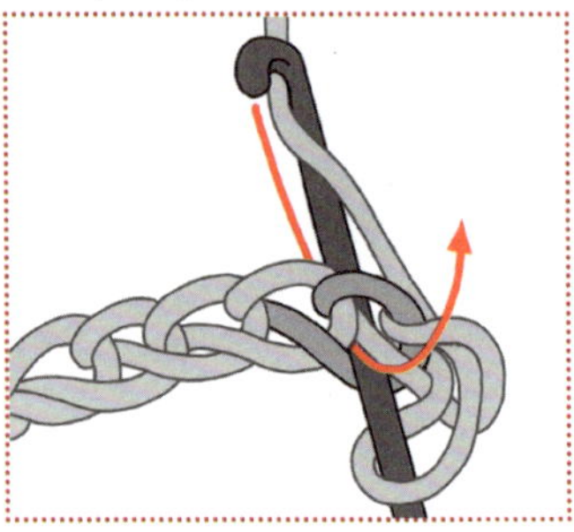

3 Hook onto the thread from behind again and pull it forward through both loops.

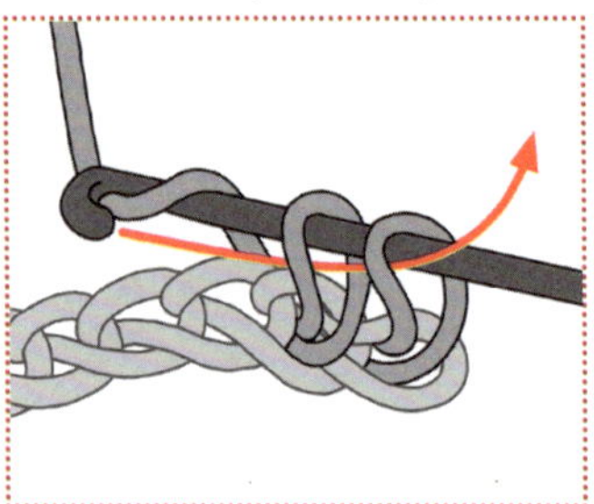

4 Push your hook into the next chain and repeat the steps.

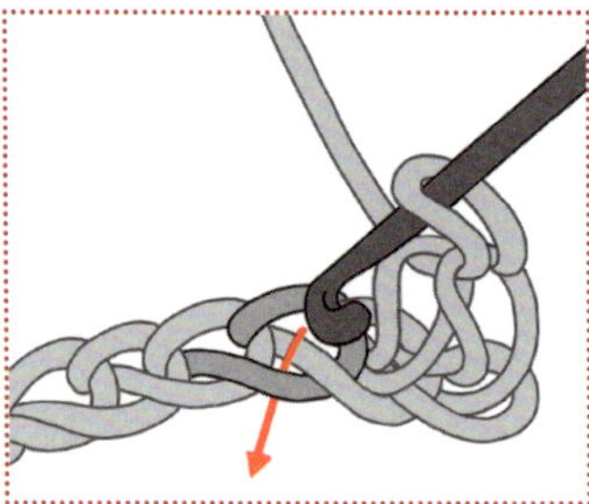

5 If you're working single crochets in rows, you will need to turn your work after each row. Always make one turning chain at the start of every row. Then push your hook into the next stitch of the previous row and continue to work single crochets.

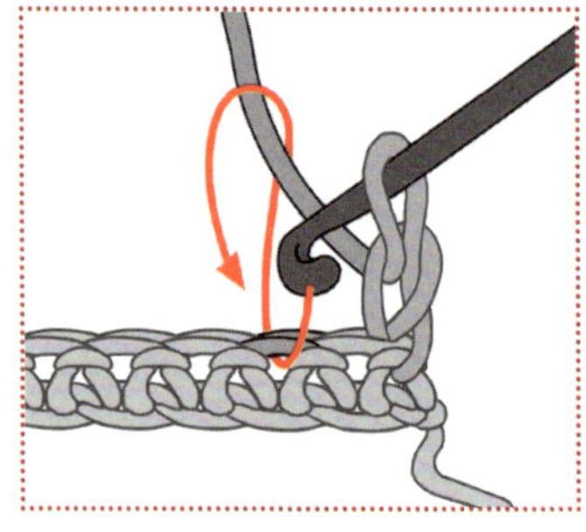

Single crochet spike stitch (sp)

1 To work a single crochet spike stitch, count two rows down from the previous row. That's where you're going to insert your hook for the next stitch.

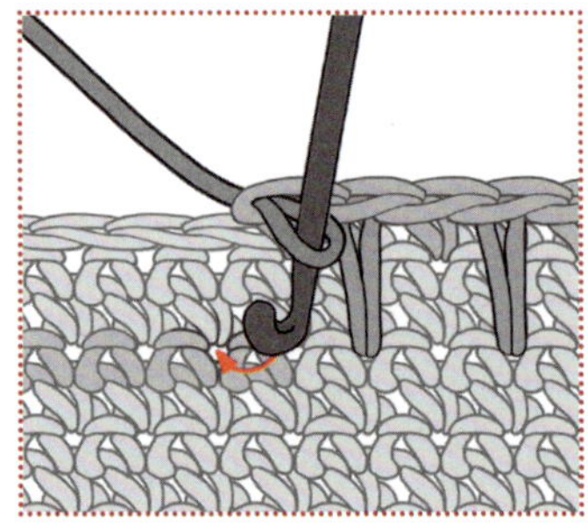

2 Pull the yarn up.

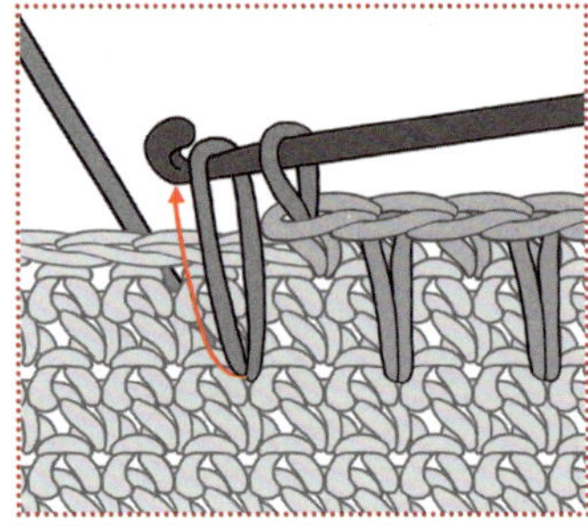

3 Pull the loop upward as far as the edge of the work.

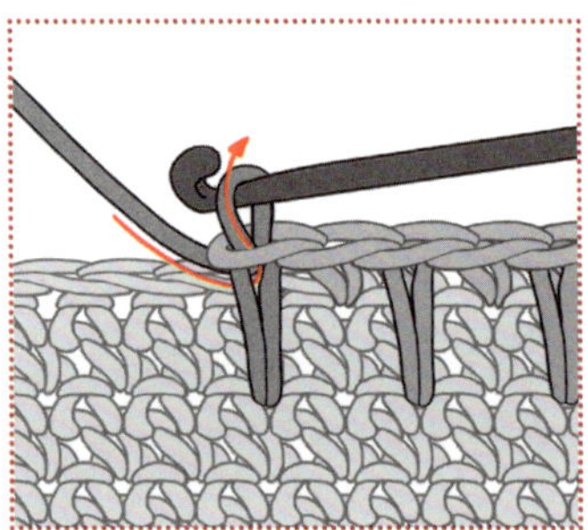

Slip stitch (sl st)

Push your hook into the next stitch and yarn over. Pull the yarn through both loops on the hook.

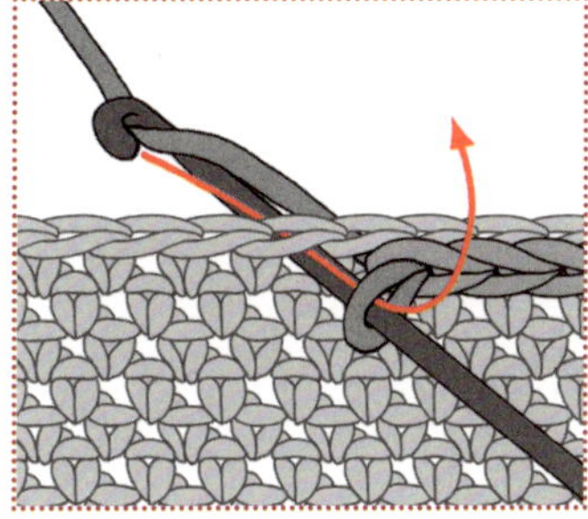

Double crochet (dc)

1 To work a double crochet, yarn over and push the hook into the next stitch of the previous row. Pull the yarn through the stitch. There should now be three loops on your hook.

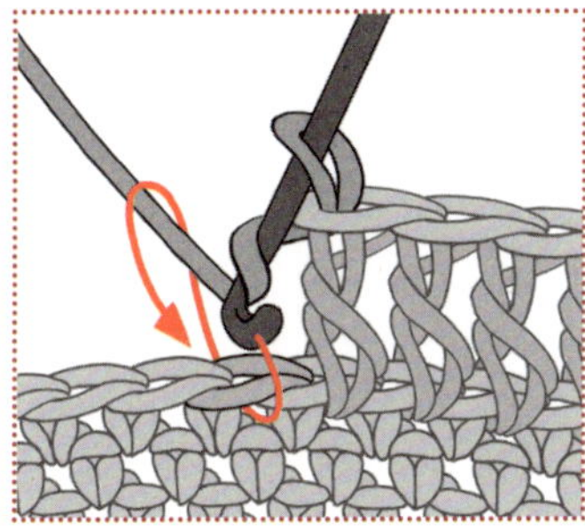

2 Grab the yarn and pull it through two of the three loops.

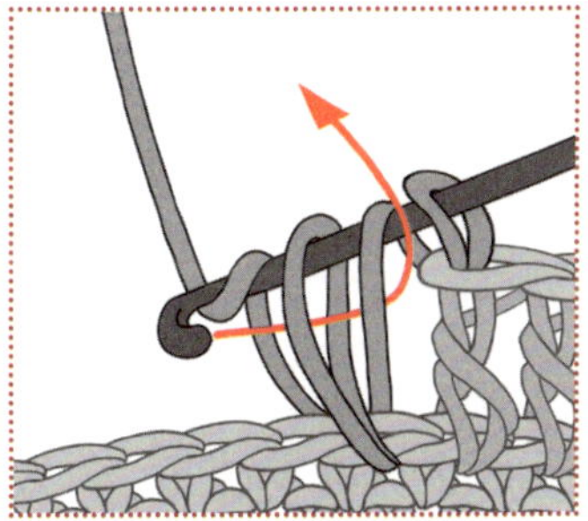

3 There should now be two loops on your hook. Now, grab the yarn again and pull it through the two loops.

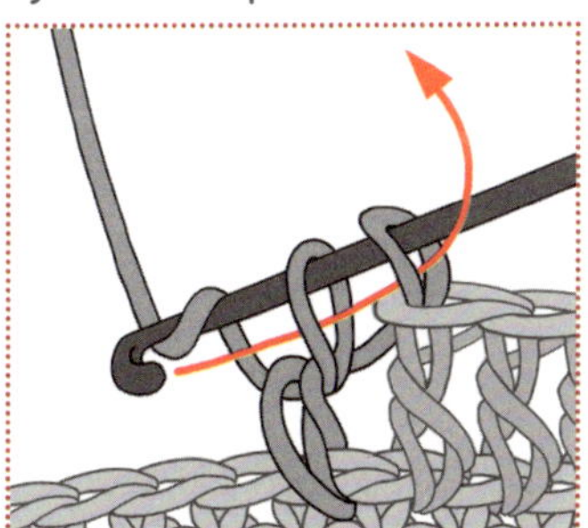

Half double crochet (hdc)

1 To work a half double crochet, first yarn over and then push the hook into the next stitch and pull the yarn through.

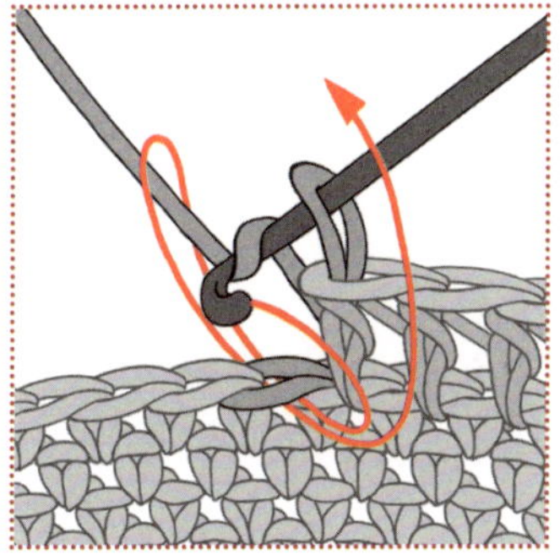

2 There should now be three loops on your hook. Grab the yarn again and pull it through all three loops.

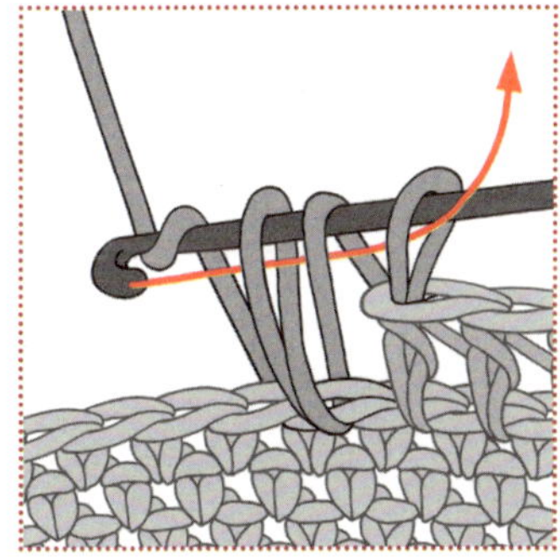

Crocheting spiral rounds

1 Work single crochets into the magic circle.

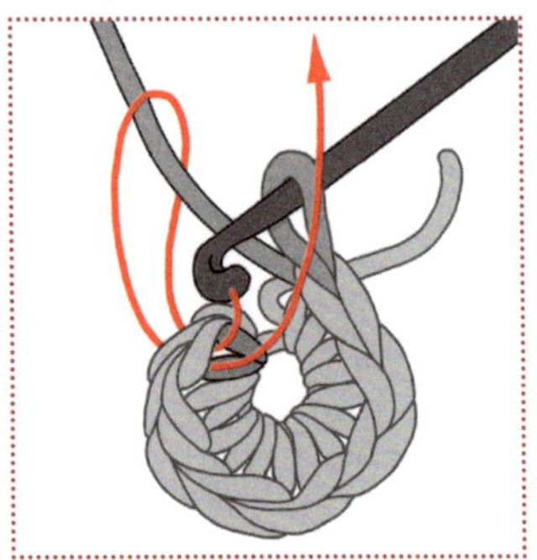

2 Place a yarn of a contrasting color between the last stitch of the first round and the first stitch of the next round to mark the start of the round.

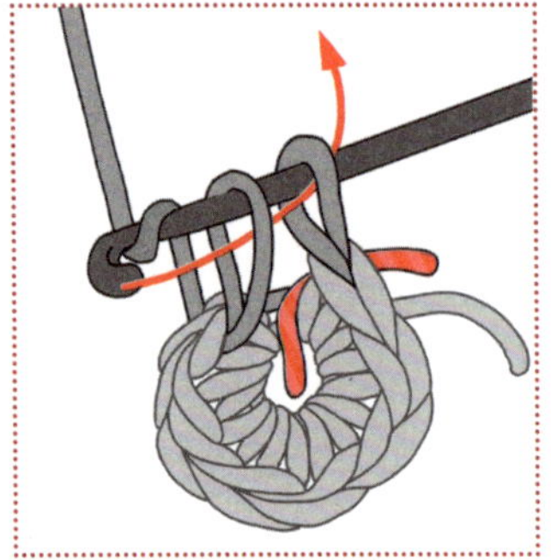

TIP: It's a good idea to insert more contrasting threads at regular intervals. Doing so will make it easier to count the rounds.

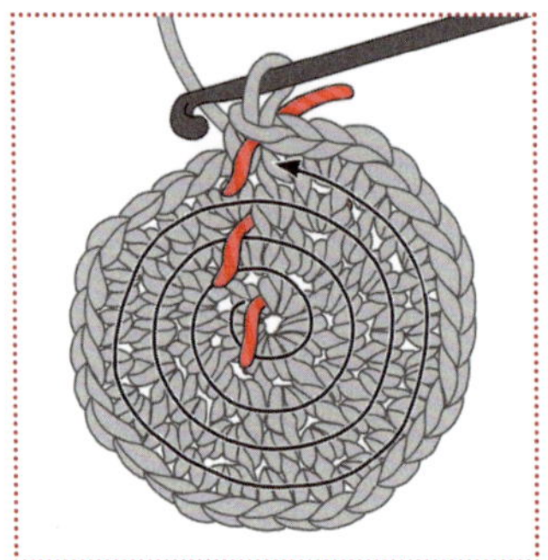

3 Once you've worked the number of stitches, pull on the loose yarn to tighten the circle. Close the magic circle with one slip stitch.

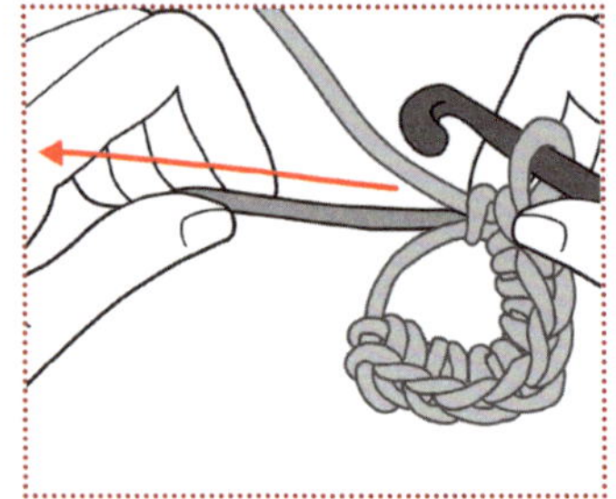

Decreasing stitches

If you need to make your work smaller or narrower, you will need to decrease some stitches.

Single crochet 2 stitches together (sc2tog)

1 If you need to decrease one single crochet, grab one loop on your hook for each single crochet.

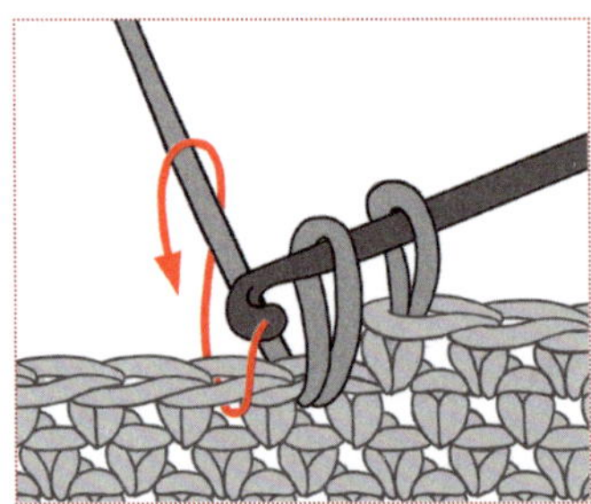

2 Then, pull the thread through all the loops on the hook. This will reduce the number of stitches by one.

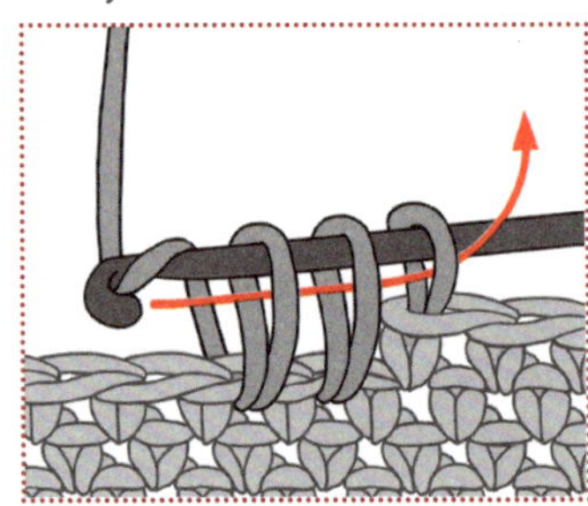

Increasing stitches

If you need to increase stitches, you can double a stitch you've already worked. In other words, you can work a second stitch in the same place where you inserted the hook for the last stitch you worked. You can use this method to increase all kinds of stitches, both in rounds and in rows. It will increase the number of stitches by one.

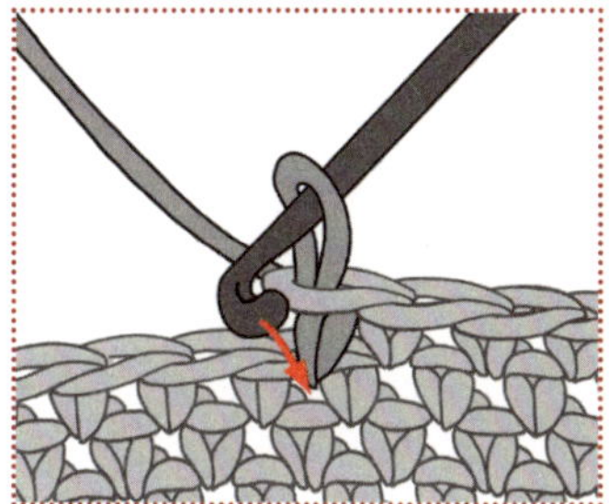

Color changes

If you need to alternate between colors for a striped pattern, pull the yarn of the first color through the last single crochet of the previous row with a yarn over so that you end up with two loops on your hook. Now pull through these two loops with the yarn in the second color. The last single crochet will be crocheted entirely in the first color and the loop on the hook will be in the second color.

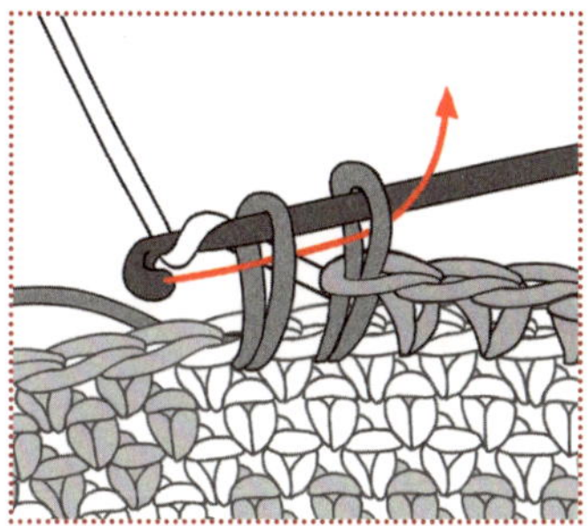

Finishing and joining sections

To finish off, cut the yarn, leaving a tail at the end. Pull the tail through the loop and weave the tail in or use it to sew the section onto another piece.

Abbreviations

ch = chain(s)
dc = double crochet(s)
hdc = half double crochet(s)
hk = hook(s)
MC = main color(s)
rep = repeat
rnd = round(s)
sc = single crochet(s)
sc2tog = single crochet 2 stitches together
sl st = slip stitch(es)
SP-2 = single crochet spike stitch worked into second row
st = stitch(es)
tr = triple crochet(s)

Notes

Notes

Notes

Notes

Notes

Notes

Notes

Notes

About the author

Annelie Kojic lives with her family in the German city of Stuttgart. She developed a love of arts and crafts at a very early age and it has stayed with her ever since. Becoming a mother led her to discover her passion for amigurumi. She began to design crocheted toys for children and continues to delight and inspire crochet enthusiasts both young and old to this day. She regularly introduces new and creative crochet designs and trends through her crochet books and her contributions as a design expert on television and in magazines. When she was diagnosed with breast cancer in 2021, crochet became the thread that guided her through the labyrinth of her illness and back into a normal life. Through her Instagram account, @bommelie_handmade, she now not only writes about arts and crafts but also speaks openly about her cancer and her journey to recovery. In doing so, she aims to give hope and courage to other people suffering from illness, because crochet is so much more than a hobby. It brings people together in its own unique way. It's a kind of yoga for the soul. In fact, it can sometimes alleviate or even prevent various side effects of cancer treatment, such as polyneuropathy.

Acknowledgments

I would like to thank everyone who made this book such a passion project for me. In particular, I want to thank my family and friends; Mareike Upheber, Lisa Braunert, Petra Theilfarth, and the whole team at frechverlag; Joanna Masiuk at Lana Grossa; and Michael Ruder at lichtpunkt GmbH.

Thanks to Lana Grossa for supplying my favorite yarn for the designs in this book.